MAGAZINE EDITING
FOR PROFESSIONALS

Revised Edition

MAGAZINE EDITING FOR PROFESSIONALS

J. T. W. HUBBARD

 SYRACUSE UNIVERSITY PRESS

Fig. 1 is reprinted with the permission of The New York Times Company. © 1912 by The New York Times Company.

Fig. 5 is reprinted with the permission of Harold Matson Company, Inc.

"THE ZANY WORLD OF ROBIN WILLIAMS" is reprinted with permission from the April 1988 *Reader's Digest.* Copyright © 1988 by the Reader's Digest Assn Inc.

"URBAN ARCHAEOLOGY" is reprinted from the April 16, 1979, *Newsweek* and is reprinted with permission of Newsweek, Inc. Copyright © 1979 by Newsweek, Inc. All rights reserved.

The excerpts from "Ted Turner's Empire" are reprinted from the June 16, 1980, *Newsweek* and are reprinted with permission of Newsweek, Inc. Copyright © 1980 by Newsweek, Inc. All rights reserved.

The paper used in this publication meets the minimum requirements of American National Standard for Information Sciences—Permanence of Paper for Printed Materials, ANSI Z39.48-1984. ∞™

Library of Congress Cataloging-in-Publication Data

Hubbard, J. T. W., 1935–
    Magazine editing for professionals / J.T.W. Hubbard. — Rev. ed.
      p. cm.
    Rev. ed. of: *Magazine editing* / J.T.W. Hubbard. c1982.
    Includes index.
    ISBN 0-8156-2463-8 (alk. paper)
    1. Journalism—Editing. I. Hubbard, J. T. W., 1935–   Magazine
editing. c1982. II. Title.
PN4778.H73   1989
020.4'1'02373—dc19   88-38503
                                                CIP

Manufactured in the United States of America.

This book is dedicated to my wife, SUSAN;
to the memory of JAMES GRANT, fine editor
and splendid raconteur; and to the spirit of
my godfather, LT. KENNETH HERRON, RNVR,
who stood the watch on the North Atlantic.

Formerly an associate editor of *Newsweek*, J. T. W. Hubbard is chairman of the Magazine Department at the S. I. Newhouse School of Public Communications, Syracuse University, and cofounder of the editorial consultant firm of Quadrant Research Associates. He has worked for *Business Week, National Geographic,* and a number of daily newspapers, including the Montreal *Herald,* the Toronto *Telegram,* and the Winnipeg *Free Press.* Also, he has published more than a hundred articles in such magazines as *American Heritage, Sail, Journalism Quarterly, Quill, American Neptune, Oceans,* and *Columbia Journalism Review.* Hubbard is the author of two other books. *The Race,* a humorous account of his experiences in the 1984 Observer Singlehanded Transatlantic sailing race, was a book club main selection. He is married with four children and, besides sailing, enjoys cross-country skiing, boat building, and collecting J. P. Morgan records.

CONTENTS

ILLUSTRATIONS

TABLES

FIGURES

ACKNOWLEDGMENTS

FOR THEIR HELP AND ADVICE in the preparation of this book, I wish to thank my colleagues in the Magazine Department at Syracuse University: Andy Fontaine, John Keats, Bill Glavin, and Bill Bender. My appreciation also goes to my colleague Jay Wright, for his advice on legal matters that arose in the preparation of this book. I also wish to thank Ed Stephens, dean of the Newhouse School of Public Communications, for his support. Special thanks also go to Bill Blair and Dick Ketchum, founders of *Blair and Ketchum's Country Journal*, for letting me visit their publication and observe their staff at work. Tom Rawls, then the managing editor of the *Journal*, was especially helpful in the preparation of chapter 10, and Bill Blair took the trouble to make some helpful and incisive comments on an early draft of chapter 12. Thanks are also due to my colleague Professor Mario Garcia of the Graphic Arts Department for reading and commenting on the contents of chapter 10. I also wish to express my deep appreciation to James Lawrence, the founder of *Harrowsmith* and *Equinox*, for his help in the preparation of chapter 12 and for his willingness to visit the university each spring and talk to successive generations of students. I am indebted to Elinor Campbell Lawrence for helping me research the early days of *Harrowsmith*. I wish to thank Professor Fred Demarest, chairman of the Photography Department at Syracuse University, and Liz Watt, Joe Cerroni, and Susan Kublick for helping me with the photographs in this book. I also wish to thank my former teacher Leonard Robinson for providing a humorous and down-to-earth sounding board for some of the ideas that went into this book. Edward K. Thompson is to be thanked for troubling to talk to me about the nature of editing. Vera Honis and Carolyn Volles of the School of Public Communications deserve a special "thank you" for helping me with administrative chores while the book was being written and then assisting me in the final preparation of the manuscript for publication. Special thanks are also due to Peter Carry, Joe Marshall, Jane Gilchrist, and Lane Stewart of *Sports Illustrated,* and to Dick Munro, chairman of Time Inc., for providing our cover picture. Finally, I wish to thank my wife, Susan Schwartz Hubbard, for her inspiration and help during the writing and publishing of this book.

MAGAZINE EDITING
FOR PROFESSIONALS

1

A NEW APPROACH
TO THE MAGAZINE

JAY CASSELL first held a fly rod in his hand at the age of fifteen. Since that moment he has been fascinated by the challenge of pursuing and — if possible — catching every kind of game fish from the feisty trout of Montana's Armstrong Creek and the largemouth bass of the St. Lawrence to the coho salmon of Lake Michigan and yet more trout in Maine's Baxter Reservation. Today Jay, now aged thirty, works hard and is paid well at his job as senior editor of *Sports Afield*, but he still cannot believe his luck.

"I've got a job where I spend my day doing what I love most. If I'd gone to work for a bank or a corporation somewhere, I'd only get a couple of weeks a year off to fish. There's no way I could have gone after bonefish in Bermuda if a publication hadn't paid the freight. I attend some of the big conventions each year, including the American Fishing Tackle Manufacturers Association's, and I know many of the top professionals in the business on a first-name basis."

Naushad Mehta, thirty-one, is a senior reporter-researcher at *Time* magazine. Since coming aboard as an editorial trainee after graduation from a prominent school of public communications she has helped research and report a great variety of stories, including covers on the assassination of Prime Minister Indira Ghandi, the Amazon basin, world debt, the composer Andrew Lloyd Webber, and a special edition about the U.S. Constitution. She has interviewed such luminaries as Dan Rather, Italian movie heart-throb Marcello Mastroianni, Bishop Desmond Tutu, and Ben Bradlee, executive editor of the *Washington Post*. Much of the magazine has to be written in the last two days of the week, which means that on Thursday and Friday Naushad may find herself working 'til 3:00 or 4:00 a.m. "It's exciting," she says, "to be right in the middle of a breaking story. It's

1

like being a part of history in the making. But it's a roller coaster, you have to get used to living with uncertainty. When you begin the week much of what you'll be writing about hasn't happened yet, and often you have to switch tracks from one story to another very quickly."

Stevie Daniels, thirty-six, is a single parent with an eight-year-old son. Yet she has found time to serve as the executive editor of *Organic Gardening*, a magazine with a circulation of one million headquartered in Emmaus, Pennsylvania. The publication, which is part of the Rodale Press publishing empire, caters to those who are interested in preserving the environment and growing vegetables without the use of artificial fertilizers. Though Stevie oversees an editorial staff of sixteen, and flies more than 15,000 miles a year as a representative of the magazine, she still has time, when she gets home in the evenings, to work the 16-by-32-foot garden plot behind her row house in nearby Allentown. "That," she says, "is how I relax."

While Jay Cassell and Naushad Mehta did not think seriously about a career in magazine journalism until they attended university, Stevie Daniels knew since high school days that this was what she wanted to do. "Fiction writing interested me from the first," she says, "but I quickly realized that journalism, with its concern for digging out the facts and telling the truth, often has more social impact. It can help people directly, and make the world a better place." The interconnectedness of things in the natural world was brought home to Daniels during an extended visit to Africa in the summer of her junior year at college. After working as a reporter on two daily newspapers and founding a natural foods co-op in Vermont, she came to work at *Organic Gardening*.

"The weird thing about this business," says Jay Cassell, "is that you can take your hobby, what you're *really* interested in, and make a career out of it. Fishing is my gig. But if I were a space nut, I'd go to work for *Aviation Week*. And if I were a sex maniac, I'd go to work for *Penthouse* or *Hustler*. It's all there, yet you hear people griping about their boring jobs and their short vacations. Geez, I may work damn hard, but I'm *always* on vacation."

In the 1950s and 1960s the larger general interest magazines were sandwiched between newspapers, with their hot pursuit of current events, and television, with its animated powers of entertainment. Many of the larger consumer books—like *Colliers, Saturday Evening Post, Look* and *Life*—bit the dust. But since the middle 1970s, changes in technology, graphics, and special patterns have enabled the magazine to redefine itself as a distinctive medium, capable of targeting in on highly select audiences with an extremely high visual and verbal impact. In the years between

1978 and 1988 the total number of magazines has increased from 9,582 to 11,229. Much of this increase has occurred in the group of publications with circulations of 500,000 or more, where the total has increased from 1,100 to 2,089 over the decade. At the same time advertising revenues for this pace-setting group have gone from $1.9 billion to $5.4 billion annually. Ad revenues for the remaining 9,000 smaller and more specialized magazines have increased at approximately the same rate to an annual total of $3.4 billion. To this total ad revenue must be added a further $4.4 billion in subscription and newsstand sales. This grand total of $13.2 billion dwarfs network television's 1987 total revenues of $9 billion.*

The economics of the magazine business, while obviously healthy, are not easily fathomed. Unlike almost any other industry, its product generates two kinds of income: ad revenues and circulation sales. This oddity can be of critical help to those intending to start their own publication (see chapter 12). But that is only half the story. Most businesses are either capital-intensive or labor-intensive. Aviation uses a lot of expensive equipment (requiring high capital investment) operated by relatively few individuals of exceptional skill. Restaurants employ a larger number of people (labor-intensive) and relatively little capital investment. But the magazine industry is unlike either of those models. "The only way to describe the magazine business," says William H. Paul, vice-president of the Magazine Publishers Association, "is to say that it is ingenuity-intensive."

Sometimes it is hard for an outsider to comprehend just how much creativity is involved. In these days of pollution controls and high fuel costs, automakers are becoming increasingly inventive. Though they produce thousands of cars each month, the top executives at GM and Ford would blow their mental circuitry if they were ordered to present 11,000 *different* models to the public at any one time. But that is exactly what happens in the magazine business. Every month the staff of each publication must design and make a product that is entirely different from those that preceded it. There is no way a transmission or a braking system can overlap into the next model; the whole book must be made over so that not a single sentence or picture is brought along from the previous edition.

Is the comparison far-fetched? Even when compared to the rival medium of television, the magazine business is unusual. The major studios produce enough material to serve four major networks. What would happen if their creative powers were called upon to produce material for

*Sources: Magazine Publisher's Association, *Advertising Age*, and *Statistical Abstract of the US*, 1988. The "totals" given in Table 898 of the *Abstract* are wildly inaccurate in that they do *not* include ad revenues for the 9,000 smaller magazines.

11,000 channels? True, the two media cannot be compared too closely; imagine what would happen if a magazine took the articles of January and April and "reran" them again in July and August.

Suffice it to say that more than just about any other business, the magazine industry depends for its continued existence upon the mental resources — the inventiveness, the good judgment, and the professional savvy — of its editors, writers, and art directors. Since the demise of *Colliers* and *Look*, most publishers have learned the lesson that if a publication is to flourish, then a proper portion of its resources must be expended upon the sustenance of the ingenious people who make this monthly miracle possible. Putting it another way, salaries for creative people are good and often downright bountiful. Today the editors of several major magazines take home more pay (with options included) than the president of the United States. A middle-level writer/editor at any news magazine could take the chairman of a small bank to lunch without feeling she'd gotten the short end of the stick. And the associate editor on one of the country's thousands of medium-sized magazines does at least as well as a competent small-town attorney.

It is the purpose of this book to help you harness your natural interests and put them in pursuit of such rewards. It is also the intention of this book to derail the teaching of the Hard Knocks School of Journalism. The chief article of faith of this fairyland institution is that you have to work for years as an editorial serf before you are competent to prepare an article for publication in a magazine. The old-timers who form the faculty of this school organize and edit material for the magazine reader by a process of "hunch" and "instinct." There is no question as to the quality of their work. It is generally superb. But if you ask the gnarled veteran why he put this quote here or that fact there, he will reply "Well . . . it just *seemed* right." Yet, when questioned further, he will deny that any knowable principle served to guide his judgments; it was just all seat-of-the-pants instinct.

We do not deny the validity of such hunches. We just assert that they are not based on thin air. In many ways they resemble the hunches some captains had concerning the whereabouts of enemy U-boats on the North Atlantic convoys in World War II. A few captains would sink one, and maybe even two, submarines on a single voyage, while the great majority of skippers had barely a nibble on their electronic detection gear. The lucky few were admired for their special gifts. But in the spring of 1941 merchant sinkings became so bad that the British Admiralty commissioned a group of scientists to analyze the problem. They found that the successful skippers had in fact based their hunches, albeit unwittingly, upon a set of procedures that could be articulated and thence applied, not by a few lucky veterans, but by all escort commanders. U-boat sinkings increased fifteenfold over a few months, and a new science called Operations Research came into existence.

There are many parallels between the problems confronting a magazine editor and those of a skipper searching for a submarine in the depths of the Atlantic. How can my limited resources be best employed? What is the most effective pattern of organization for this story? Where, in this ocean of verbiage, can I discover the best words for my headline? This book applies the principles of Operations Research to the problems of magazine writing and editing. Such an approach may not be too popular with the Hard Knocks School of Journalism, but we have found it to be singularly effective in preparing several generations of Syracuse University students for careers in magazine work. So far, there are no reports of sunken submarines, but just about all our graduates have gotten the kinds of jobs now held by the three young professionals mentioned at the beginning of this chapter.

2

WHAT MAKES
A GOOD STORY GREAT?

T HE PERSONALITY OF A MAGAZINE must be firm and distinct. Yet it can also be as quirky and as subtle as that of any human being. In an important sense a good magazine *is* a human being — the conjoint personality of its editors saying, "Yes, we want this article" and "No, not for us." If a magazine is healthy, its columns will crackle with confidence and energy. If it is sick, it will drag around the house in a long bathrobe, boring its readers to death with talk about the good old days. If it is *very* sick, the publisher may order it onto the operating table for major surgery; and there, like the old *Saturday Evening Post*, it may expire under the knife.

Free-lance writers are often perplexed and infuriated by what seems to be the choosiness — or plain caprice — of magazine editors. Article ideas seem to be accepted and rejected without reference to any understandable criterion of judgment. Take the case of *Harper's* and *Atlantic Monthly*. To the uninitiated they seem to have the same editorial personality. Both have circulations of several hundred thousand and both are aimed at well-educated people with strong social and political concerns. Tweedle Dum and Tweedle Dee? Not a bit of it. A writer may labor for months over an article for *Atlantic,* only to have it rejected. "Witty, well-researched, and wholly original insights into the White Slave Trade"—they like to let you down lightly—"but definitely not for us." Send the same piece off to *Harper's* and receive a note by return: "In all my years as an editor it has seldom been my privilege to read such a perceptive and provocative piece on the White Slave Trade. This is definitely for us."

THE WINDOW

The free-lance writer may attribute such contrasting responses to editorial whimsy. But in a more thoughtful mood he or she may realize that both editors probably know their jobs quite well. The ability to determine precisely the kind of information, service, and entertainment that readers expect is a vital part of any magazine editor's skills.

When American astronauts return from space their shuttle must pass through a one-mile-square "window" in the sky. If the shuttle comes in too low, it incinerates in the atmosphere. If it comes in too high, it bounces back into space. In the same way, when an author shoots an article at a magazine its trajectory must pass through that window in the sky. If it doesn't — no matter what its appeal — it will simply burn up or bounce off into space.

A good magazine editor must have a very clear feel for the location of the window for his or her publication. If an editor is vague about its position, and accepts material that flies wide, he or she is likely to cause severe damage to the personality of that magazine. The sedate readers of *Foreign Affairs* do not expect to find "Six Ways to Make It with a Married Man" in their October issue, any more than the readers of *Iron Horse* (a flesh-stacked motorbike magazine) expect to be told how to construct a birdbath in their back yard.

Just pinpointing the editorial window is not enough. Far more article possibilities pass through that window than any magazine can publish. An editor must therefore also develop the ability to decide which articles are most suitable and which are less suitable. The ability to compare and judge between two stories of competing merit is a very important journalistic skill. Each day newspaper editors must decide which stories shall be played on page one, which shall go on an inside page, and which shall be dropped.

For newspapers, a story topic cannot pass through the editorial window if it does not have one or all of these editorial criteria:

1. Impact
2. Timeliness
3. Prominence
4. Proximity
5. Conflict
6. Bizarreness*

*See list in Melvin Mencher, *News Reporting and Writing*, Wm. Brown, 1981, pp. 70–74, and a similar list offered by Brian S. Brooks (et al.), *News Reporting and Writing*, St. Martin's Press, 1980, pp. 6–7.

Magazine editors can employ the same criteria, but they are only useful up to a point. Their readers want to be entertained and informed, but they also want to be helped with their problems and made more skillful in their hobbies and jobs. Much of daily journalism derives its appeal from the criteria of timeliness and proximity. "Geewhiz, this event (murder/strike/fire) happened in my city today!" The fleeting appeal of such material is underscored by the truism that nothing is as stale as yesterday's newspaper. I once worked for a large city daily that ran five editions each afternoon. The format required the staff, even on the leanest news days, to top itself every 45 minutes. It was no easy trick, and our headlines used to run like this:

2:15: TWO MEN SLAIN IN BARBERSHOP SHOOTOUT

3:00: WOMAN, 20s, SOUGHT IN DOWNTOWN KILLING

3:45: MYSTERY WOMAN ESCAPES BARBERSHOP DRAGNET

Such self-destruct journalism is fine for a swashbuckling metropolitan daily of the old school. It has impact (violence, blood), conflict (murder), proximity (our city), and timeliness (today, now). But there is absolutely no way a magazine, a single issue of which may take months to prepare, can work with these criteria of journalistic value.

A NEW CRITERION

What characteristics, then, make the more enduring stories — the kind a magazine can handle — interesting? To answer this question let us take a close look at the anatomy of one of the great stories of the twentieth century. Like many other major stories, the sinking of the *Titanic* on the morning of April 15, 1912 made its immediate impact upon the public mind in the form of a newspaper account (see fig. 1). But if we analyze the events of that day purely in terms of newspaper values, we only obtain half the story. On this level, we get:

1. Impact. More than 1,200 people died in the accident.
2. Timeliness. The *Titanic* sank hours earlier.
3. Prominence. Casualties included such noted Americans as John Jacob Astor and Benjamin Guggenheim.
4. Proximity. The disaster may have occurred in mid-Atlantic, but surviving witnesses landed at Boston and New York.

Fig. 1. The *Titanic* disaster.

5. Conflict. Many male passengers were forcibly prevented from entering the lifeboats.

6. Bizarreness. Some male passengers are said to have donned women's attire to obtain places in those lifeboats.

The sinking of the *Titanic* clearly meets the criteria laid down for an exciting newspaper story. But it is more than that. How is it that, more than half a century later, the events on that night in April 1912 hold a continuing fascination for the American public? For years, major magazines ran articles about the event. Several successful movies and television dramas have been built around the sinking of the *Titanic,* and Walter Lord's well-researched book *A Night to Remember* has run through more than thirty printings since its appearance in 1955. What is so memorable about the *Titanic?*

Let's take a closer look at the dramatic ingredients of the disaster. The foreword to Lord's best seller confronts the reader with some perplexing insights. It seems that in 1898, some fourteen years *before* the *Titanic*'s disastrous maiden voyage, a man named Morgan Robertson wrote a novel about a huge new ocean liner that, with a passenger list of glittering celebrities, struck an iceberg one April night. Fourteen years later (i.e., in 1912) the White Star Line actually constructed a liner like the one in Robertson's novel. Both leviathans were some 800 feet in length, and had triple screws that could push them along at 25 knots. Each ship carried three thousand people, but lifeboats for only a fraction of that number, since both liners were deemed to be "unsinkable." The White Star Line dubbed its real-life ship the *Titanic.* Fourteen years earlier Morgan Robertson, with eerie precision, had named his doomed monster the *Titan.*

What is it that raises the goose bumps on the back of your neck? There is a mystery and a paradox here. How can a man writing a novel in 1898 foretell, almost down to the name of the ship, one of the great disasters of recent history? But the paradoxical element extends far beyond Robertson's prediction. The *unsinkable/sinks. Beautiful* people/suffer *ugly* death. We also see the unquestioning heroism of upper-crust male passengers who decided to go down with the ship so that women and children of almost no social consequence could be assured of a place in the lifeboats. Old Ben Guggenheim wandered off to his cabin and dressed in white tie and tails for the final dip. It is hard to imagine one of today's Beautiful People in similar circumstances surrendering his place in the lifeboat; such gallantry is barely credible now. Yet it happened.

Paradox. The dictionary defines paradox as a "seeming contradiction." This criterion is not mentioned in the six categories for the judgment of newspaper stories. Yet it is clearly a major ingredient in the enduring drama of the *Titanic* and its sinking. The seeming contradictions raise question marks in the mind of the reader, and it is the desire to resolve those questions that fuels the reader's interest. Without the discovery and delineation of that paradox, the reader's mind would surely have glazed over in a maze of detail about lifeboat capacities, courses steered, and the precise locations of the *Titanic*'s slowly flooding stairwells.

BLACK HOLES

A paradox holds an enduring fascination for the human mind. Children love them. When is a door not a door? When it's ajar, silly. Few adults are immune to their allure. Who among us is not intrigued by the astronomical fact of black holes? An entire star can be sucked out of time itself into one of these cosmic sinks. The cataclysmic event becomes even more intriguing when the astrophysicists tell us that the same stellar matter is instantly regurgitated elsewhere in the universe. There are mathematical equations to prove it. But for ordinary people the idea that such a thing can happen remains a haunting paradox. Perhaps this is why a recent issue of a national news magazine, featuring a black hole on its cover, confounded the bums-and-boobs stalwarts by breaking that year's record for newsstand sales.

When a magazine editor is reviewing article ideas, trying to discern which might go and which might not, he or she would do well to consider the element of paradox. It explains the ongoing appeal of many big stories. Why did Edward VIII give up his throne for a homely divorcee from Baltimore? How did John Kennedy, the most elaborately protected man in the world, come to be shot with a mail-order rifle? How could the Reverend Jim Jones convince nine hundred people to drink poison and end it all in the swamps of Guyana?

These, from a journalistic point of view, are the superstories. But the same principle holds true for less dramatic articles. There is a paradox inherent somewhere in their material, and if the magazine editor exercises shrewd judgment he or she can bring it out, put it high in the story, and use it as a catalyst to fuel the reader's interest through the more routine parts of the piece. Here is an example:

> Two years ago David Smith, aged 22, had both his hands blown off in a flying accident. Yet today he can drive a car, sew on buttons, and make delicate repairs to his TV set. Thanks to a phenomenon known as myoelectricity . . .

The situation of a man with no hands who can still perform these delicate tasks forces the reader to ask: Why? How is that possible? And before you know it he or she is deep into the body of story. Here is another example of the use of paradox in a relatively routine story:

> West Germany finished World War II as a heap of rubble, her capital city held in thrall to the new superpowers. She had few natural resources of her own. Yet today, the Federal Republic boasts one of the most stable and prosperous economies in the Western world.

The reader is compelled to ask: How is that possible? How can something come from nothing? Soon he or she is deep into the intricacies of Germany's postwar economic "miracle."

If magazines are to surmount the problems imposed by slow publication schedules and lack of geographic proximity (the obverse of which form the basic ingredients of "geewhiz"journalism), then their content must concern itself with matters of enduring appeal. As we have seen, from the sinking of the *Titanic* to the mass suicides in Guyana, much of this appeal seems to stem from the fact that the riddle, the seeming contradiction, holds an unquenchable fascination for the human mind.

When editors sift story ideas, they would be well advised to seek out those stories that evoke a strong element of paradox; it is these articles whose appeal is likely to be most profound and most far-reaching. Spotting this element of apparent contradiction is not always easy, but it is a skill of fundamental importance to aspiring magazine editors. Our first assignment is devoted to developing this skill.

ASSIGNMENT

Make a list of the ten most dramatic stories of recent years, and see if you can identify any paradoxes that might be lurking at the center of their popular appeal. Here are three openers, just to help you get the list started:

1. Watergate and Nixon's resignation
2. The sexual exploits of televangelists
3. American schools' failure to compete with those of other industrial nations
4. ???

Answers

1. Man of *major power* unhorsed/for *minor flaws*—a common theme in Shakespearean tragedy
2. They don't *practice* what they *preach*
3. World's *richest* country/runs *poorest* schools

TOGETHER
THEY SPELL *SHIP*

HE EDITORIAL OFFICES OF *Country Journal* MAGAZINE occupy the
second floor of an eighteenth-century wayside tavern on the
outskirts of Manchester, Vermont. It is a blustery, cold day in
November and Dick Ketchum, the founding editor of the trendy back-to-
the-earth magazine, is presiding over an editorial meeting.

Tom Rawls, his husky young managing editor, and Jake Chap-
line, the associate editor, settle back in their green-cushioned wicker chairs
around Ketchum's desk. Several years ago Ketchum and William Blair, the
publisher of *Country Journal*, quit successful careers in Manhattan and
"retired" to the hills of Vermont. Ketchum's office is like that of one of Norman Rockwell's small-town attorneys. Pre-Revolutionary political cartoons,
hand-colored, decorate the walls. In his previous existence as an editor of
American Heritage magazine he wrote, among other books, an account
of the battle of Bunker Hill and a biography of Will Rogers. Now a picture
of Rogers hangs behind Ketchum's desk. Beside it is a poster of a Mafia
don flanked by three dark-suited musclemen. "When I want your opinion
I'll give it to you," declares the hard-faced capo.

"That's supposed to intimidate the staff," Ketchum glumly informs
a visitor. "It doesn't work." The poster certainly does not deter Rawls and
Chapline from arguing a couple of points quite fiercely with Ketchum.
The meeting is important, for even now the April issue — four and a half
months away on the far side of winter — is taking shape.

"It makes sense," declares the bearded Chapline, "to do a compre-
hensive service piece on all the federal and state programs that can help
you harvest and sell your woodlot." Wood stoves, and the creation of
wood for them, are an important topic for *Country Journal* readers.

"Yeah," Ketchum replies somewhat skeptically, "but John [a writer]

Fig. 2. Old Wayside Tavern in the village of Manchester, Vermont, serves as editorial office for *Country Journal.* Business offices are 40 miles across the mountains in Brattleboro, near the home of *Journal* publisher William Blair.

is already doing a piece on the New England Forestry Foundation. Wouldn't there be an overlap?"

"But that doesn't tell the reader how to do it for himself," objects Chapline.

Rawls interrupts. "How about a sidebar of 750 words on federal and state programs?" The discussion continues, but Ketchum runs an open shop and by both policy and temperament is reluctant to force an opinion on his subordinate editors. Instead, the Mafia boss is allowed to scowl down from the wall in disgust and the story idea is put on hold while Chapline finds out more on how the piece on the Foundation will go.

"How's the rest of April look now?" Ketchum asks of nobody in particular. The editors attempt to build a core of five or six articles into the heart of every issue and then add material as space permits. Ketchum's question about the April issue hangs in the air, and managing editor Rawls goes over to a notice board propped up beside Ketchum's desk. It is divided into twelve vertical columns, one for each month. All article ideas are given a 3" × 1" white or blue card and stuck into the most appropriate

Fig. 3. Richard Ketchum (right), the founding editor of *Country Journal*, presides over monthly editorial meeting with managing editor Tom Rawls (left) and associate editor Jake Chapline. Storyboard, with breakdown of articles of months ahead, stands on table behind Ketchum.

monthly column. The nature of its subject matter requires *Country Journal* to follow the seasons with particular care.

By this date in mid-November, the February column is pretty well locked up. March is solid, while April, May, and June are still in the process of formation.

"For April we've got a solid how-to — how to plant an apple orchard," says Rawls. "And to go with it as our centerpiece we've got a great picture story on old-time apples. Illustration is mostly color paintings of apples the way they used to be." The issue also contains a personality profile on the Tcherneys, a husband-and-wife team who illuminate manuscripts in the monastic tradition. For a balanced core April also needs a natural history article (it promptly receives a piece on kingfishers) and what Ketchum calls an "issue piece" — something on a topic of pressing importance or interest to country dwellers. It may concern an inhumane new method of pig farming, acid rain, or the savage encroachment of farmland by suburban development. Sometimes, it can even deal with a bright new trend for the country dweller.

So far, April does not have an issue piece. There is some talk of bringing forward from the June column a story on a black farm couple in Alabama. The story is a good one and contains a significant element of paradox. Many programs designed to help the black farmer in the South seem, in fact, to have the reverse effect. After some talk, the black farmers stay in June — they may be the cover for the issue — and the search for April's "issue piece" continues.

"We have to be careful about these," says Ketchum. "Many of our readers turned to rural life to be rid of problems. Often, they just don't want to hear it. But some problems relate directly to their interests, and I feel they should know about them." Ketchum is so confident of what his magazine stands for, of the location of its editorial "window," that he is prepared to disturb his readers a bit with his articles.

The editorial meeting continues. Finally, a human interest story on a successful garden cooperative located amid the craters of New York's South Bronx is selected as the issue piece. The message to readers is clear: Even in the urban moonscape of the Bronx, not all flowers are born to waste their sweetness upon the desert air; in short, there may be hope for city folk after all. Now the final pieces are fitted into the jigsaw of the April issue. These include a second service piece on how to increase garden fertility by relocating pathways in the yard.

Country Journal is rightly proud of its service pieces. "They, as much as anything, distinguish us from *Yankee* magazine," says Ketchum. "Our readers are actively working the land and want more than just nostalgia, though they are interested in that too." One of *Country Journal's* more successful articles was a piece entitled "What on Earth Is a Pung?" The pung, it turns out, is a kind of old-time sled noted for its surprising efficiency in hauling firewood over rough terrain. The story contained diagrams of how to build and use one.

Most of Ketchum's employees have a strong interest in the land. Often a story idea will spring from their own experience, or difficulty with, say, a problem with organic fertilizer, or the legalities of fence building. If they are having the problem, then a large number of readers may also be wrestling with it.

When the meeting is over, the April edition of the magazine has pretty well come into focus. However, as we shall see later in chapter 10, by the time January rolls around some of today's careful arrangements are going to come unstuck. Besides containing some eight regular columns (readers' letters, a note from the editor, a recipe column, a poem, a column on vegetable gardening, and so on), the issue will also contain nine and maybe ten articles, depending on how much space is available after advertising has been sold. All the articles must be appropriate for the *Country*

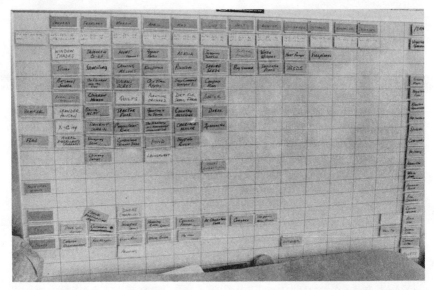

Fig. 4. Storyboard for future issues of *Country Journal* as it stood at the end of November editorial meeting. As we shall see in chapter 10, the lineup of articles for the April issue underwent substantial change in the process of production.

Journal reader; all must pass squarely through the magazine's editorial "window." Yet while the April issue must resemble previous issues, it must also contain a few surprises. "Offering a change of pace without jolting the readers is a major challenge for an editor," declares Ketchum.

CONTENT AND FORM

In the editorial meeting we just sat in on, we saw a new issue of the magazine coming to life, taking shape within the limits imposed by the needs and interests of the readers. We saw the editors discussing a broad range of articles. But they were not merely concerned with the subject matter (*content*); they were also discussing the way (*form*) in which that subject matter could be presented to the reader.

Content consists of all the facts, statistics, and quotes that go into a story. The writer assembles them through a process of research and interviewing. The *form* of presentation, from the editor's point of view, is much more complicated. It does involve style, the way a writer puts words together. But even more important, it involves a judgment about the kind of story the editor chooses to present to his readers. This concept becomes clearer if we think of the neutral facts being poured into a mold. When the material is tapped out of that mold it may be in the form of a "how-to" article, or in the form of a personality profile. There are four major kinds of article form:

1. Service
2. Human interest
3. Informative-news
4. Personality profile

It is easy to remember this list because the initial letters form the word SHIP. This mnemonic is not a quiz-time gimmick; when an editor is confronted with a mass of confusing information on a topic, there is a natural tendency to lunge at the material and force it into the first article form that comes to mind. This lunge, however, can be a great time-waster. The editor may rip a dozen half-filled sheets of paper from his typewriter in frustration before he realizes the error of his decision. Much better to whisper the word SHIP and, in a moment of suspended judgment, cooly review *all* the possibilities of form for a particular mass of material.

In the monthly editorial meeting we saw the editors of *Country Journal* talking about all four of the basic story categories, as well as some less fundamental forms.

Service or How-to Articles

Examples of service pieces are the stories on how to plan an apple orchard and how to build a pung. This kind of article is the workhorse of magazine journalism. Few newspapers are prepared to risk alienating their general readers by giving them detailed advice on how to improve their tennis backhand, or boost the output of their ham transmitter. Most are not tennis players, nor are they radio operators. Such pieces would, however, have an obvious appeal for readers of *Tennis World* and *QST*. The specialized magazine audience has a nearly insatiable appetite for enlarging its knowledge and skills in its specific area of interest. We've all seen them. Seven Ways to Improve Your . . . Soufflé/Shooting/Sex Life/Sewing/Samba.

The *service* or *how-to* article has an affiliate that might be called *opinion-review.* The writer's opinion is clearly involved, and it generally takes the form of telling the reader what to buy and what not to buy, which play to attend, and which political candidate to vote for or against.

The Human Interest Piece

The *Journal's* human interest pieces include the stories about the greening of the Bronx and the farmer in Alabama. This kind of piece generally concerns the affairs of unknown people who must come to terms with a situation (good or bad) that is not of their making. Instead of numbing the readers' minds with tables of statistics about urban decay, or the difficulties black farmers are having in Alabama, the *Journal* takes the stories of ordinary people and presents the difficulties in personal, human terms. If a personality profile can be said to describe little things about big people, then a human interest story is big things about little people.

The big thing may be a storm that takes a score of lives, or the winning of the $1 million lottery by a gas station attendant. But whatever the great peril or great joy, it is not set in motion by the abnormal abilities of those involved; the moving cause is external.

Informative-News Article

The article on kingfishers is an example of a *news-informative* piece. It is not telling the readers how to do anything, nor is it inspiring them with the deeds of ordinary people in an extraordinary crisis. It is simply retailing information that has no other purpose than to enrich the life and the knowledge of the reader. The process of purveying simple information for its own sake is the preoccupation of the newspaper medium. The productive time lag for most magazines makes it difficult, if not impossible, for them to compete in this arena. However, there are two informative subforms that magazines use very effectively. They are the *exposé* and, perhaps the most challenging of all stories to organize, the *trend.* True, the former of these does have a tinge of opinion-review in its makeup (e.g., throw the rascals out). But the trend is generally plainly informative. It may concern a trend in evangelical religion, portrait painting, or massage parlors. The thought that the reader may be a part of the trend, or invited to join it, is generally well submerged.

Personality Profile

The piece about the couple who illuminate manuscripts with such artistry that the White House has been among their clients is a personality profile. In this form the subject of the story must be noted for some special achievement brought about by the exercise of individual talent. The person may be famous, as in the case of Marlon Brando or Neil Armstrong. Or he or she may be an unknown who has achieved something notable. Not many people have heard of Professor Varian Fry. Yet it was this man, a professor of classical languages, who, at the request of President Roosevelt, went to France in the early 1940s and arranged by many deceptions to hustle hundreds of refugees out of Europe to America, right under the noses of the Gestapo. Though his name is hardly a household word, Fry's deeds are exceptional and his success is a product of his courage and his guile, and he is thus amply qualified to be the subject of a personality profile.

The profile concerns itself with little things about big people. The readers probably know about Brando's success in *Streetcar Named Desire* and *The Godfather*. What they want to hear about is what time he gets up in the morning, what kind of Scotch he drinks, and how many eggs he had for breakfast.

ASSIGNMENT

Read the following data sheet through carefully. It is an intentionally mixed-up "data-mash" of information concerning a new kind of medical cure. When you feel you have a good grasp of the material, outline drafts showing how you would present it (probably to different audiences) as (1) a service or how-to piece, (2) a human interest piece, (3) an informative-news piece, and (4) a personality profile. The purpose of this exercise is to show how the same material can be poured into a variety of molds and presented to specific readerships.

DATA-MASH ON ELECTROMEDICINE

Beth Ganz, age eight, had her spine curvature reduced from 38 degrees to 15 in six months by Dr. Bobech. Before, she had to lie on her bed eighteen hours a day, and be fed by hand. Her only interest was watching TV. Now she can feed herself, ride a bicycle, bake cookies, and play with other kids between classes. She has an IQ of 131 and likes cats and stamp collecting. Her father, Ted Ganz, is an accountant. He says: "This treatment has transformed Beth from a vegetable to a lively, active schoolgirl. It's a miracle." Dr. Bobech came to North America from Hungary in 1956 and received his medical degree from McGill University. He has published many distinguished papers on his research into muscle spasm, and twelve years ago was appointed executive director of the Toronto Electro-Medicine Institute. He has four children of his own. He and his wife Else, whom he met while interning in New York, like to play golf and chess. The doctor is also an amateur gardener, and has developed a new strain of tomato called the Buda; it ripens in two-thirds of time, and has a sharp, rich taste. It is extremely popular in Canada, with its short growing season.

A lot is written about miracle drugs these days, but one of the most miraculous cures of all is achieved by something that is not a drug at all. It involves the harnessing of small amounts of electricity. It is generally called Electro-Medicine, and serious research is being done in New York, Paris, and in many cities across Canada. The leading researcher is generally regarded as Dr. Michael Bobech at Toronto's Hospital for Children. A team of doctors under Bobech places radiolike devices about the size of a silver dollar just below the rib cages of young children with abnormally curved spines. On orders from a transmitter, electrical pulses — usually about 10 microamps — are sent to the dollar-sized electrodes implanted in the afflicted muscle tissue, thereby stimulating and relaxing them. Bobech began his research in 1970 on animals, but the treatment was so gentle and so effective he began to use it on children with scoliosis. Many with spine curvatures of 10 and 15 degrees were cured within six months.

Last April 23, Bobech took on his biggest challenge of all: Beth Ganz, who had a spine curvature of 38 degrees. After six months of treatment this was substantially reduced. Equally small electrical currents are being used to cure bones that won't set, wounds that won't heal, epilepsy, bedsores, skin ulcers, unknit bones, and amnesia. At St. Barnabas Hospital in New York, Dr. Walter Fennimore is using a tiny brain-pacer for patients with drug-resistant epilepsy. One twenty-six-year-old man, who suffered uncontrollable seizures daily, had no trouble after the pacemaker was put in. With a grant to the Necker Hospital in Paris, the U.S. Army is researching into techniques of sending wounded soldiers to sleep without the use of drugs. Small currents are passed through the brain from electrodes attached to the head by a metal band — something like that in Frankenstein movies. Teams of nerve doctors at UCLA are helping accident victims regain use of limbs by using minute pulses of electricity. Other researchers at the University of Washington, Seattle, have discovered that electronic stimulations of the thalamus region of the brain can eliminate amnesia and help long-term memory. It is rumored that electromedicine may eventually produce a cure to multiple sclerosis. One day Dr. Bobech was working in his lab in December 1971. (He is a broad, burly man who looks somewhat like an elephant; his hair is slicked back in the slavic manner.) Bobech realized the connection between minute quantities of electricity and muscle spasm by inducing a spinal curvature of 18 degrees in a laboratory pig; if one can cause curvature, he reasoned, one can surely cure it. This was the start of his research into problems of children with spinal curvature. So far he has treated effectively more than 100 kids.

Solutions

1. Service piece to mothers in, say, *Parents* magazine on how they can get treatment if their children have muscle problems. Alternatively, a piece written for doctors in a medical journal on how the new techniques can be applied.
2. Human interest piece of Beth Ganz, how this changed her life. Big events about little people. She did not devise the cure; it came from without. Such a piece may go well in *Reader's Digest* or *Redbook*. It would also present a fine vehicle for explaining, in direct human terms, the new technology.
3. Informative-news article would have to be about some recent development by one of the researchers, for instance the case of research to end amnesia, the Necker hospital results, or the recent rehabilitation of Beth Ganz. Such a piece might well appear in the medical sections of the newsweeklies *Time* and *Newsweek*. It might also form a trend.
4. Personality profile might well be an article on Dr. Mike Bobech, the kind of man he is, how he made his discoveries, his hobbies, his home life. Once again we have a fine vehicle for explaining the details of the new achievements in human terms. But unlike the human interest story, this will include little things about a big person. Such a piece could well form a profile in the *New Yorker* or a cover story in the newsweeklies and a multitude of other publications.

4

EDITORS AND WRITERS
Story Ideas, Outlines, and the
Book of Bad Beasts

T HE RELATIONS BETWEEN WRITER AND EDITOR have always been stormy. Way back in the spring of 1775, Robert Aitken, a Philadelphia printer and editor, hired an out-of-work English drifter named Thomas Paine to write for his *Pennsylvania Magazine*. Paine's brilliant and provocative commentaries gave a strong lift to circulation. But as time passed Aitken had increasing difficulty persuading Paine to pick up his quill and get down to work. Once, the editor became so desperate to get his hands on Paine's latest article that he sought out the writer in his lodgings in the slums of Philadelphia. Paine had not even started the project. Aitken grabbed him by the shoulder and compelled him to sit down "at the table with the necessary apparatus, which always included a glass, and a decanter of brandy." The eyewitness account continues:

> The first glass of brandy set him thinking; Aitken feared the second would disqualify him, or render him intractable; but it only illuminated his intellectual system; and when he had swallowed the third glass, he wrote with great rapidity, intelligence and precision; and his ideas appeared to flow faster than he could commit them to paper. What he penned from the inspiration of the brandy, was perfectly fit for the press without any alteration, or correction.*

Since that time generation upon generation of editors have by turns coddled and hounded their writers into creativity, and writers have responded with their own characteristic blend of enthusiasm and truculence. In any

*Frank Luther Mott, *A History of American Magazines* (Cambridge, Mass.: Harvard University Press, 1938).

joint literary venture nerve ends are liable to get rubbed sore. But in the realm of magazines, the problem is sometimes exacerbated by the tendency of both writers and editors to hold a perverse view of the others' contributions.

The writer, from the editor's standpoint, may seem a spoiled child who keeps no office hours, travels where and when he or she chooses, and can make big bucks with a single two-hour celebrity interview. To the writer, editors often seem to be overeducated personages of independent means who go about their editorial duties in the mode of Eustace Tilley: luncheon at the Plaza, then afternoon sherry with Aunt Ithelda. Almost incidentally, somewhere between these engagements the editor decides whether the poor writer shall dine at Burger King or feast at Maxim's. And even when a manuscript is accepted, much of the fun evaporates through margin comments like "Awkward, rework" and "MEGO" — mine eyes glaze over.

THE LUNCH EDITOR

There are, it is true, a few well-tailored exquisites still extant. One news magazine still supports a Diplomatic Editor who does little more than haul visiting dignitaries off to elegant receptions and dinners. In the same vein, a noted woman's magazine has a sleekly groomed lady editor who never writes a line but devotes her time to buttering up book publishers in the hope of obtaining rights to excerpt their latest hits. Her working colleagues irreverently refer to her as the Lunch Editor.

Most magazine editors, however, do not lead the charmed existence dreamed up for them by writers. Instead, they inhabit a pressure tank in which the push to get the magazine out and to make each issue better than the last never ceases. Each month ten, twenty, or even thirty relevant and exciting article ideas must be unearthed and prepared for publication. Just as the March issue starts to take form a plaintive cry can be heard: "But what have we got for April?" Deadlines must be met. Artwork must be commissioned. Instead of having audience with his tailor, the real-life editor is likely to be found closeted with the magazine's business manager trying to figure out next month's "draw"— the excess of press run over paid circulation. And instead of sipping champagne at the Plaza, that editor will find himself gulping a beer and a pastrami in a corner tavern with the associate publisher, and getting hell for last month's 11 percent cost overrun.

The working editor, if the magazine is to be a success, must have three basic skills. First he or she must have an imagination that is capable of generating a continuous stream of plausible story ideas. Those ideas must not just fly around in outer space. They must fit the publication's editorial format; they must pass, if you like, squarely through the magazine's editorial "window."

Second, an effective editor must have or be able to develop a far-ranging acquaintanceship with writers and their varied battery of skills and interests. Asking Tom Wolfe to cover the Miss America contest might be fun. But would he agree to do it? How much would he charge? And would the reader be amused? And, if Wolfe does not want the job, whom else do we have?

The third primary skill of the editor is the one that generates the steam. He or she must be able to take the finished manuscript and edit it so that it meets the readers' interest without, if humanly possible, crushing the writer's style. Occasionally manuscripts, like those of Tom Paine, sail through without need of alteration or correction. But more often both rearrangement and partial reconstruction are necessary. This process may constitute a "scissors and paste job," the straightforward realignment and fine-tuning of clearly presented material. Or it may comprise a complete overhaul, where the editor reworks the entire piece from top to bottom. On rare occasions the original idea just does not work out and the editor must scrap the whole project and pay the writer a "kill fee"—generally about 20 percent of what the author would have received if the piece were published.

The qualities that make a good magazine editor often differ from those that make a good editor of books. Max Perkins was undoubtedly one of the most talented book editors of this century. He discovered and nurtured such legendary talents as those of Scott Fitzgerald, Ernest Hemingway, and Thomas Wolfe. Yet his modest assessment was that an editor serves, at best, as a "handmaiden" to authors, helping them by one means or another to release their literary energies. While magazine editors may take quite a bit of trouble to encourage their writers, there is a clear point at which the handmaiden defers to the bite of passing time. "The editor is the guy who has to make up his mind," declares Edward K. Thompson, the founder of the highly successful *Smithsonian* magazine, and for many years the chief editor of *Life*. "He has to become arbitrary at a certain point, or the magazine would never get to press."

Sometimes the decisiveness necessary for the effective functioning of any magazine appears to be mere caprice. Harold Ross, the founding editor of the *New Yorker*, so mistrusted the precepts of modern psychology that he banned the use of such words as "introvert" and "extrovert"

in his magazine, along with the most harmless jokes about relations between the sexes, which he haughtily dismissed as "bathroom and bed-
room stuff."

Rarely do the three primary editorial capabilities — ideas, assignment, presentation — reside in equal strength in a single individual. An ac-
quaintance of mine once served as an editor of a confession magazine. He
could dream up story ideas with aplomb.

THIRTEEN — AND PREGNANT AGAIN!

MY UNCLE SEDUCED ME — ON MY WEDDING NIGHT!

MY HEART WAS TRUE, BUT MY BODY NEEDED DOUBLE LOVING.

These tag lines, when placed on the cover of a magazine, would give a
fine boost to newsstand sales. But such is the structure of the "confession"
piece (heartrending trouble, followed by an upbeat solution) that my friend
frequently could find no writer capable of creating an upbeat conclusion
for the lurid predicaments into which he'd plunged his characters. Result?
No story. Clearly my friend was a most fertile source of story possibilities,
but he lacked the editorial insight required to discern which ideas would
fly and which ideas would defy any kind of happy resolution.

It is a fact of life that magazine editors frequently find themselves
working in an area that does not make full use of their particular interests
and talents. An editor whose prime interest is the environment may find
himself spending his time editing stories about sports. While I was at the
National Geographic I was assigned to work on a story about the mating
dance of an orange parrot that dwelt in the jungle of South America. I
have never been very interested in birds, but I worked hard, and the piece
came out so well that all subsequent bird stories alighted upon my desk
and I, much to my annoyance, became something of an expert on the blessed
things. The classic case of editorial miscasting, however, occurred when
Harold Ross hired a gentle and unassuming writer named James Thurber
not to write but to run a mythic Central Desk that would ramrod the work
of all the *New Yorker*'s artists and editors into some semblance of order.
Some of the disasters that were visited upon this misappointment are charm-
ingly described by Thurber in his memoir *The Years with Ross*.

Generally, however, an effective chief editor will attempt to match
up talent and interest with position. An editor with a particularly fertile
imagination should oversee the generation of story ideas. Another, adept
at making drab copy sparkle, should handle presentation. And an editor
with a shrewd knowledge of writers and their particular capabilities should
be placed in charge of handing out assignments. Sometimes this wisdom

is built upon a lifetime of bumping shoulders with people in the business, and sometimes it is discovered in the contents of a file-card box. When Otto Friedrich, the author of *Decline and Fall,* the classic inside account of the collapse of the old *Saturday Evening Post,* took over as foreign editor of that magazine he was startled to be handed a little green box, and told "Everything is in here." And it was — everything from the name of every foreign correspondent who had worked for the *Post* in twenty years, to every government source who might have any insight on overseas events, including the name, address, and home phone number of the anonymous colonel who served as a spokesman for the CIA.

IDEAS

Now let's look at the three basic editorial functions in more detail. Story ideas are the lifeblood of any magazine. As a rule some 80 percent of them are generated by the editors, and the remainder come in over the fantail from agents and would-be writers. The ideas must not be so outlandish as to blow the average reader out of his socks. And neither can they be so predictable as to wrap the reader in a cocoon of boredom. Steering between these alternatives is no easy task. In the cynical view of the managing editor of a major men's magazine, the perfect story idea is one that "skims down the far side of next year's cliché." The ability to spot such esoterica is a subtle art that generally combines an awareness of popular social trends and a profound knowledge of the magazine and the interests of its readers.

A new editor hired by a magazine is generally told to study back issues and "think story ideas." Such instructions are easy to give and often impossible to follow; the newcomer cudgels his or her brains for hours, or even days, and draws a blank. How can an editor overcome this block?

I once got some insight on this problem from the American entrepreneur Daniel K. Ludwig, reputed to be the world's richest man. At the time I was working for *Business Week.* We knew Ludwig had a hearty dislike of publicity, but his achievements were the stuff of myth. His nondescript holding company, National Bulk Carriers, controlled more shipping tonnage than any other shipowner in the world. NBC mined iron ore in Australia, dredged rivers in India, built new cities in the jungles of South America, managed the largest orange grove in Panama, and operated two of the grandest hotels in Bermuda. Ludwig's colossal projects are the envy of less successful men; they gaze upon his achievements, beautiful in their simplicity, and wonder why the same idea has not occurred to them.

"How do you get your ideas for new ventures?" I asked Ludwig in his offices at National Bulk Carrier in midtown Manhattan. At first Ludwig was reticent. Then he said: "An idea looks different before it is developed. It takes a different set of antennae to identify a possibility before it has become a reality."

I suspect this insight is also true of story ideas. An unwritten story (represented, let us say, by the shape of a triangle) looks very different from the finished article in the magazine (represented, say, by the shape of a diamond). A writer or editor may read back issues of a magazine most assiduously and fail to attune his eyes to the shape of a new story idea. The problem is that he is trying to spot diamonds when he should be searching for triangles.

Antennae

Developing the antennae to spot an unwritten story is a difficult process. Much of it, I suspect, is a product of trial and error, of seeing some ideas pan out and others, superficially of equal merit, bite the dust. Most writers agree that there is a magical moment encountered in the preparation of any major story. After they have devoted a significant amount of energy to research, the idea stirs, rolls over in its sleep, and awakens into some wholly unexpected new form. Sometimes the story rolls right out of bed, and has to be killed. On other occasions it is transformed into a far better and more exciting story than anyone imagined. That moment, when previously quiescent material takes on a life of its own and begins to emit a host of new research possibilities, is one of the most exciting experiences a magazine writer can have. He or she follows the trail into unperceived possibility; small surprise, then, that the end product bears little or no resemblance to the original idea.

If a story idea is to work for a magazine, then it must fly through the "window" prescribed by the editorial format. When an editor thinks story idea, the location of that window must be as clear as the framed Wyeth or Winslow Homer hanging on the office wall.

"Who are my readers?" asks Andre Fontaine. "That's the central question." Fontaine is the author of the book *The Art of Writing Non-Fiction*, has served as an editor for such magazines as *Collier's* and *Redbook*, and has been a successful free-lance writer for more than twenty years. "What are the readers' interests?" he continues. "How do they live?

What are their concerns, their problems?" Answer these questions, says Fontaine, and you are well on the way to obtaining a good story idea. Perhaps the readers have trouble paying their kids' college fees? Or pruning their cherry tree? Or is it that their *ragout suprême* tastes like donkey dung? Any one of these can form the basis of an excellent story idea.

Often the problem or situation is one in which the writer has been entangled. Perhaps it was his *ragout* that stuck to the pan. Or her cherry tree that came creeping into the upstairs bathroom one night. If the writer has the problem, then perhaps many others have it too.

John Keats, a lifelong free-lancer and author of more than a dozen books, approaches the problem from this direction: "I think in terms of what interests me," he says. "I'm confident that I'm more like other people than different from them, so if something interests me, it interests a hell of a lot of other people." Keats recognizes that his idea may not go for a specific magazine, but he trusts that if it is effectively presented there should be a roost for it somewhere.

No one can think of great ideas in a vacuum. To generate a fertile selection of story ideas, editors must cultivate a variety of interests. A daily newspaper is essential reading; add to this a wide range of magazines. But one must not only keep up with developments. The aspiring editor must be able to leap ahead of them, and get on the far side of those aborning clichés. To do this an editor must often pursue her interests into the technical and scholarly journals. If she wishes to generate ideas in the business world then she must read *The Harvard Business Review* and the *Wall Street Journal*. "If you're looking for good ideas on medical topics," declares William Glavin, formerly an associate editor and top medical writer for *Good Housekeeping* magazine, "then you should read publications like the *Lancet* and the *New England Journal of Medicine*."

Cross-pollination

Some of the best ideas, in and out of journalism, come from the cross-pollination of interests and skills. When two compartments of knowledge are brought into interaction, each can undergo a major change. In recent years much of archaeology has been revolutionized by the advent of aerial photography and the use of infrared film. In the same fashion, modern physics is receiving a strong epistemological boost from the teachings of Zen Buddhism. On a more modest scale, a writer with a firm knowledge of sociology and the intricacies of silicon chip circuitry can propound some unnerving insights into how our society will look in the year 2000. Similarly, a journalist versed in the nuances of modern radio astronomy might have some stimulating thoughts to offer on the future of our pictorial art.

There are days, however, when your imagination closes down altogether. The fight to the commuter train or to the subway, and the first strong drink at the end of the day, become the only realities your mind can grasp. When this happens, an aspiring magazine editor should know that there is still hope — there are still a couple of devices for getting the juices flowing again. Skip over the headline stories in the newspaper. These have, in a sense, been "mined out." Take a look at the one- and two-paragraph notices that fill the bottoms of the inside columns. Here's an item about a Yale medical professor who's been reinstated after he weathered charges of academic plagiarism. A story idea? What is plagiarism? Does it happen often with the pressure to publish or perish? How is it dealt with? Are there some dramatic historical instances? Does the nature of modern research require a new definition? Here's another one. An airline pilot wins a $250,000 libel suit against his own airline; it had charged he was going nuts when he claimed that the airline's explanation of a crash was false. Is there a piece on air safety here? Are pilots and flight controllers still dangerously overworked? Why? Do crash inspectors tend to blame pilot error rather than black box navigation devices? Why?

I culled those story ideas (cross my heart) from the first newspaper I picked up, the *New York Times* for November 13, 1980. The task is a relatively simple one, once you attune your antennae. There is one other standard way of jogging the imagination into creativity. Check the Yellow Pages of the phone book. Humankind devotes one-third of its day to sleeping, one-third to goofing off, and one-third to the business of making a living. Somewhere in the backs of our minds lurks the thought that if one isn't a test pilot or a white mercenary or a journalist, one must lead a pretty dull existence. But the Yellow Pages prove otherwise. The endless kaleidoscope of human occupations must jog a corner of your imagination. How about a piece on a school for barroom bouncers? How about an article on the sixteen agencies that will rent you any kind of animal from a panther to a pelican for your TV commercial, or your offbeat cocktail party? Fortunetellers? Just check the entry in any major American city, and away you go!

HANDLING THE WRITER

The second primary skill of the magazine is the ability to select a writer with the appropriate skills and then guide and inspire that writer into submitting an acceptable manuscript on deadline. We shall discuss the third primary skill — editing and presentation — in subsequent chapters.

Sometimes the selection of a writer is straightforward. If a writer who is technically competent and well-versed in the field of medicine comes up with a story idea on new wrinkles in organ transplants then, quite simply, he or she deserves first shot at the assignment. Most ideas, however, are generated in-house and it becomes your task as editor to discover a writer who is capable of tackling each particular assignment. Experienced editors generally have a card file of writers who have worked well in the past; often this is cross-referenced by specialty. If you have just begun work on your magazine, the *Directory* of the American Society of Journalists and Authors (1501 Broadway, Suite 1907, New York, N.Y. 10036) should be a great help. It lists most of the professional free-lance writers in the country by name, giving address, home phone, and a bio of professional accomplishment. At the back of the *Directory* the names are broken down by speciality: Economics, Folk Craft, Outdoors, and so forth.

The editor selects a likely name and broaches the idea. If the writer has sold a number of pieces to the magazine already, then he or she will not need an extensive briefing. But if this is the writer's first effort for the publication, then editor and writer should get several matters clear:

1. What approach, or angle, should the article take (service, human interest, informative, personality profile, or what)?
2. How long will it be?
3. What is the deadline?
4. Will any artwork be required?
5. What about payment? Expenses?

These are five basic determinants of any assignment. The writer may wish to bring his agent into the discussion — if he has one — particularly on questions of payment and expenses. When mutually agreeable terms are reached, it is in the interests of both parties to sign a contract, or at least to get the major points into a letter of agreement. If this is a maiden effort by the writer for the publication, he or she may also ask the editor:

6. Do you have tearsheets on a story with similar treatment and approach appearing in a recent issue of the magazine?
7. Can we discuss the project again when the research has been completed?
8. Will you review the opening paragraphs of my final manuscript to see if I'm on track?

You, as editor, may have no objection to these additional requests. But here is a warning. If you grant them you become enmeshed in the creation of the article and you will find it increasingly hard to subsequently reject it. If you are confident about the article's acceptability, fine. But if you are not, you should make your misgivings plain to the writer from the start. The editor who waxes enthusiastic about a story right up to delivery, and then rejects it, has a special place reserved for him or her in the Bestiary of Bad Editors.

Story Outlines

As an editor you may get a query on what sounds like a great story idea, but you are not quite clear as to how it would work out. In such a case it is appropriate to request a story outline from the writer. This should run three or more pages and contain a sample lead and a detailed account of research and interviews planned. Generally, story outlines are used in negotiations with established writers, or when a hefty advance or expense money is involved. If a writer who is not established has a good idea, he or she will be told: "Good idea, but we'll only take it on spec." Translated, this means the writer will get paid if the magazine likes the final manuscript. If it doesn't, the writer gets zilch, plus an "interesting" experience.

So far we have discussed the formal side of editor-writer relations. Creation, even at its simplest, is a mysterious process. An editor can serve as a writer's inspiration, sounding board, critic, mentor, punching bag, friend, loan shark, and taskmaster. There ought, in an important sense, to be a marriage of talent between a good editor and a good writer. "A good editor is capable of a kind of dual vision," says Leonard Robinson, an editor at the *New Yorker* who became managing editor of *Esquire* and later head of the magazine sequence at Columbia University. "He or she must be able to understand, from an inside perspective, the problems that confront the writer. At the same time the editor must keep a clear eye on what kind of material will best serve the interests of the magazine, and its readership."

Reconciling these two perspectives is not always easy. Sometimes an editor must act as a stern overseer, as when Robert Aitken stormed through the slums of Philadelphia and yanked Thomas Paine out of his lodgings. And on other occasions editors must court the writer's muse with compliments, and decant glass upon glass of expensive brandy—or its equivalent—so that the writer, like Paine, can get his thoughts in gear.

THE BESTIARY

But sometimes relations sour. A writer talks up a piece on which he or she cannot deliver. Research is shallow. Deadlines are missed. Most good editors (Aitken's manhandling of Paine notwithstanding) treat their writers gently, even when they have strong reservations about a particular piece of work. But some do not. They use their power not for the benefit of the magazine — though that is often their excuse — but to let their own egos out for a romp at the writer's expense. In the Bestiary of Bad Editors the biggest cages are occupied by four basic ogres. It is hoped that you, as an editor, will not come to resemble any of them.

The Butcher

This individual views the writer's finished copy as raw meat that can be hacked and chopped into any shape, so long as it bears no resemblance to the version submitted by the writer. Chances are that Butcher will be slashing away at the manuscript before he has read it through once. Butcher knows best. The writer has by definition got it all wrong, and if any sentence or phrase can be changed, then it will be. Butcher, bloody up to the elbows, warps the story into an inferior dimension by stripping out all the best quotes and insights on the grounds that they are "over the reader's head." Giveaway quote: "Now, how can we cut another fifty lines out of this . . ."

The Flasher

This editor, sometimes also known as the *Marshmallow Marine*, comes on strong and likes to propose hard-hitting sock-it-to-'em projects. "Let's take a no-holds-barred look at Pentagon cost overruns/city hall corruption/organized crime." The writer, often at some peril, pulls the piece together. The Flasher slaps his fist into his hand and yells, "Great, great!" But when the article goes into galley proofs, Flasher has a tendency to open his raincoat and show these proofs to the sources interviewed. These persons, lying through their clenched incisors, promptly deny ever having said any such thing. Flasher, with a triumphant smirk, then takes the offending passages out of the story. Giveaway quote: "Now if we could only get the Pentagon/city hall/organized criminals to confirm these allegations . . ."

The Perpetual Tinkerer

This kind of editor may well have bold ideas and be a fine editorial craftsman, but he or she can never quite believe the writer's research, and thus is always calling for more interviews and yet more research. When the research is triple-checked, and documented into the ground, Perpetual Tinkerer now likes to rework the copy — after politely seeking the writer's approval — and rework it yet again. Unlike the Flasher, he or she does not shy away from tough stories; it is simply that he is also a perfectionist in a highly competitive catch-as-catch-can business. Giveaway quote: "Frankly I just don't think the readers will buy that in its present form."

The Gargoyle

This editor is the most insidious beast of all. Like his ancient namesake, he is known for his sphinxlike appearance and his ability to hang off roof-gutters for long periods of time without committing himself. When a writer submits final copy to him, the dialogue goes like this:

> GARGOYLE: I don't like it.
> WRITER: Why don't you like it?
> GARGOYLE: I stinks. Rework it.
> WRITER: But what's wrong? Is the lead bad, do I need more stuff on the subject's childhood? Or what?
> GARGOYLE: Jesus, how should I know? It just needs a hell of a lot of work.
> WRITER: But how can I rework it if I don't know what's wrong with it?
> GARGOYLE: It's your story, baby.
> WRITER: (Probably emboldened by the Kafkaesque flavor of the exchange) But you're the editor.
> GARGOYLE: Yup, I'm the editor, and I say it stinks. Rework it.

Two days later the writer returns, hollow-eyed, with the revised manuscript in hand. The Gargoyle leafs through it, feet on desk. Then, after a sharp intake of breath, he speaks.

> GARGOYLE: It still stinks. Tone it up some more.
> WRITER: But how . . . , etc.

On reading dialogue like this, the aspiring magazine editor may be filled with disbelief. It is hard to credit that Gargoyle, together with fellow ogres

Butcher, Flasher, and Perpetual Tinkerer, actually exist out there in the editorial world. But they do, and some of them have parlayed their troll-like talents into quite sizable salary checks. The last three Beasts in the Bestiary lack a basic ingredient: editorial courage. In the case of the Flasher and the Perpetual Tinkerer, this is the lack of courage to trust the writer they have hired. For Gargoyle, it is a lack of courage in his own judgment. If the story is criticized higher up in the pecking order, the writer can be held responsible. In contrast, old Butcher has, if anything, too much courage. He is a primitive, rushing in to cut away any flourish of originality, thereby reducing all to the lowest common pablum.

If you should encounter any of these creatures in your editorial career — and you almost certainly will — it is best to handle them with a kind of wry circumspection. And when you, in your turn, achieve a position of editorial eminence it is hoped you will know enough to stay well clear of the Bestiary.

5

THREE WAYS
TO START A STORY

ARISTOTLE, THE CELEBRATED GREEK PHILOSOPHER, was born in 384 B.C. in the North Aegean city of Stagira. His father was a doctor and the boy learned the arts of dissection under his tutelage. By the time he arrived in Athens to study at the age of seventeen, Aristotle had developed a fascination for collecting and classifying all phenomena in the world around him. He made lists, among other things, of plants, shellfish, bugs, dreams, the winners of international gymnastic competitions, human dispositions, geological strata, and city constitutions. When Alexander the Great, his former pupil, conquered most of the known world and much beyond, he decreed that hundreds of researchers in the new lands send their specimens and discoveries to Aristotle back in Athens. Eventually, the philosopher became so knowledgeable about the world of nature that Dante, writing one and a half thousand years later, described him with adoration as "The Master of Those Who Know."

But despite his reputation for Olympian wisdom Aristotle made, in the course of his work, some classic bloopers. He failed to make an accurate count of the legs of an ordinary spider, and consequently categorized it as an insect instead of an arachnid. Learned men held Aristotle's judgment in such esteem that the poor spider was not classified aright for more than a thousand years. Though Aristotle was undoubtedly one of the world's great biologists, his scientific acumen sometimes fell apart when it came to human beings. It was his strong belief that men and women were more likely to conceive a child in winter because that "was when the wind blew from the North." This quaint notion of human procreation is quite overshadowed by Aristotle's ambiguous view of human morality. His *Nicomachean Ethics* is a classic of starchy rectitude — yet it was dedicated to his only son, the product of an illicit but long-

37

standing love affair between the Master of Those Who Know and a slave woman named Herpyllis.

The preceding paragraphs were written as something of a game. No, none of the material is false; it is all amply documented in the scholarly biographies of Aristotle. It is simply that the cited facts have been organized into one of the classic patterns — or leads — used by editors to introduce the central subject matter of a magazine article. Indeed, if magazines had been around in Aristotle's day, he undoubtedly would have collated and classified the various types of article leads, along with his gymnasts, his bugs, and his municipal statutes.

When material is presented in such a form the reader is most curious to know more. Aristotle, generally perceived as a sanctimonious old bore, suddenly comes to life. We are anxious to know more about the Master of Those Who Know, the lissome Herpyllis, those mysterious North winds, and even that tiresome and almost unreadable treatise on ethics. Such are the foibles of humankind; and such is the art of the editor in presenting them.

THE CHICKEN/EGG PROBLEM

The lead of a magazine article has special importance. It is prime time — so much so that some writers will devote as much as a third, or even one half of their writing time to its creation. If the focus of the introductory sentences is wrong, then the reader won't understand what the article is about. And if it is right, but boring, the reader will toss the magazine aside. An effective lead must both arouse the *justifiable* curiosity of the reader and foretell something of what lies ahead.

From the writer's standpoint, much of the challenge — and difficulty — in the business of creating leads stems from a version of the chicken/egg problem. How can I write a good lead to a story, the author may ask, when I don't know how the pieces of my story are going to be organized? And how can I organize the pieces of my story when I have no clear notion of how it is to begin?

A good magazine editor can help a writer resolve such mind-bending dilemmas by viewing the entire project from a more distant perspective. "This is a great piece," the editor might be able to say, "but I think your lead is probably lurking in the anecdote that starts in your fifth (or fifteenth) paragraph."

To make such judgments an editor must have a clear understanding of the strengths and limitations of particular kinds of leads, and how each kind relates to the problems of story organization. A number of distinguished journalists-turned-teachers have labeled and categorized all the different kinds of leads known to the world of magazine editing. Some of these latter-day Aristotles have suggested what we might term the "literary classification," which categorizes openings by the kind of language used, narrative, descriptive, and expository.* Others categorize leads by the mode in which the data are physically presented on the page: summary, striking statement, bam-bam-bam, and anecdotal.** All of these are useful divisions but, from the standpoint of the magazine editor, I would suggest a different form of classification, one that emphasizes the way in which each kind of lead seeks to arouse the interest of the reader. Basically, under this functional form of classification, we see that there are three primary types of lead. They are:

1. The startling assertion lead, plus general statement
2. The round-up (or bullet) lead, plus general statement
3. The indirect lead, plus general statement

I have attached the concept of the general statement to each kind of lead because it is an integral part of constructing any effective introduction to a magazine story. The general statement identifies the main theme of the article. This, it announces to the reader after he or she has been dazzled by the fancy footwork of the lead, is an article about an antiwhalehunting group, or an article about an Arabian king who executed his granddaughter for adultery. Often, I have found, aspiring editors devote great care and imagination to crafting an elegant lead, and then leave it hanging without any bridge into a central theme. That lead may move very fast but, like the Red Queen in *Through the Looking Glass,* it never gets anywhere.

Before we take a closer look at the basic type of lead, we should note that all the most beguiling stories, from a journalistic point of view, derive their appeal from an underlying paradox, a seeming contradiction. A good editor will seek to bring out this inherently dramatic element. If he or she can *validly* incorporate that sense of paradox into the story's lead, it can then serve as a catalyst to fuel the readers' interest through the more routine parts of a story—or perhaps, even, through a dry Aristotelian treatise on right moral conduct.

*Betsy P. Graham, *Magazine Article Writing* (New York: Holt, Rinehart & Winston, 1980).
**André Fontaine and William A. Glavin, Jr., *The Art of Writing Nonfiction,* (Syracuse University Press, 1987).

THE STARTLING ASSERTION

In its simplest form this kind of lead simply confronts the reader with an unexpected fact or statement. Here are two examples and the general statements which they introduce:

> Early in 1979 five women at a chemical plant in Willow Island, West Virginia, made public the fact that they had had themselves sterilized in order that they might keep their jobs . . .

GENERAL STATEMENT { These cases dramatize an extremely complicated and emotional issue.

Redbook, March 1980

> No one in Washington likes to talk about U.S. military satellites, on or off the record. National security, you understand. . . . Forbes has learned, however, that U.S. military satellites are not only watching Russians — they're watching us too.

GENERAL STATEMENT { At present, this sharing of information between defense and civilian agencies is less sinister than silly. But left unchallenged it has potential for serious mischief, as one company, Dow Chemical, has already learned.   *Forbes,* May, 12, 1980

> Are you faithful, darling?
>
> The answer to this question is always yes, says my friend who lives in Paris. "But, of course," he goes on, over a scrumptious lunch of stuffed roast lamb with wild mushrooms at Maxim's, "Europeans know better than ever to ask that question. It is just assumed that monogamy is rare, if not impossible, among lively people, and the question never comes up."

GENERAL STATEMENT { Whether my friend's observation is true or not . . . it certainly does seem that Europeans see marriage differently than Americans do.

Elle, July 1988

These three leads present a straightforward and highly dramatic way of getting the reader into a story on voluntary sterilization, a story about how the Pentagon keeps tabs on private industry, and a yarn about European attitudes to marriage. The element of paradox in each is explicit, there for all to see. Writing such leads is relatively straightforward once that paradox has been exhumed from the raw materials of research.

But there is a far more subtle version of this kind of lead, one in which the seeming contradiction is implicit rather than explicit. Often this form of startling assertion plays off a well-known aphorism. For instance, when introducing a story about the awful state of the national economy, we might write the following:

> The economy, declared one of the president's top advisors, is going to get worse before it gets worse.

Such an assertion generates an implied resonance with the familiar saying that things are going to get worse before they get better. The reader is startled into a kind of double take. Such leads, with their ingenious play on words, can be among the most challenging of all to compose. Here is another:

> It is not who you know but what you know that counts in the field of nuclear engineering.

Such a lead might get you nicely into a piece about how, in the wake of the Three Mile Island disaster, nuclear power authorities are becoming less politicized and more safety-minded. Sometimes the implied counterpointing can be even more veiled, but nonetheless effective, as we see in this delightful opening to a Russell Baker column in the *New York Times Magazine.*

> As a product of the American educational system, I may not know anything about history but I know what I like, and one thing I'm crazy about is the French Revolution. It was one revolution that had everything: those wonderful guillotines . . .
>
> *New York Times,* July 31, 1980

Behind the Bakerian irony lurks a clear counterpoint with the Babbitty declaration "I may not know anything about art, etc. . . ."

Startling assertion leads are fine for getting into a straightforward story fast. But this kind of lead has its limitations. It is generally not too effective for opening the more complex trend story, and it lacks the human touch generally required for the personality profile.

THE ROUNDUP (OR BULLET) LEAD

This kind of lead is particularly effective for getting into a story that involves material scattered across time or geography. It has also been called a bullet lead, or bam-bam-bam lead, for the nuggets of information it spits, machine-gun-like, at the reader. It is particularly effective for getting into a trend story, since a trend generally involves a lot of small changes taking place across a wide spectrum of endeavor, be it in the world of art, housing, or political attitudes. Taken on their own, these changes are inconsequential, but together they become significant as a trend. A roundup or bullet lead seeks to highlight a spread of these changes, then links them to a general statement on the nature of the trend. Here is an example:

> Wendy's is putting salad bars in its hamburger restaurants. McDonald's is presenting the McChicken. And Burger King is looking for an entree to breakfast.
>
> GENERAL STATEMENT { Far from being the start of a new wave of fast-food expansion, those moves actually are efforts to keep customers coming in the door. After 25 years of nonstop growth, fast-food sales stood virtually still last year — setting off strident competition for a stagnant market.
>
> *Wall Street Journal,* April 4, 1980

The three bullets — Wendy's, McDonald's, and Burger King — come at the reader fast. Together, they lay the groundwork for the general statement that they are competing fiercely over a stagnant market. In some roundup leads the general statement precedes the bulleted items, but the effect is the same. Also, on some occasions the number of bulleted items rises to four or, very occasionally, drops to two. Here is a charming example of the former:

> They have cut their engines, stopped pedaling, feathered their oars, switched on the cruise control. In short, they have put their feet up. All around them, others are still sweating to make a mark, but not the Coasters.
>
> GENERAL STATEMENT { Coasters can relax. They've done it. Gliding happily along on reputations made years and years ago, they remain squarely in the public eye, status only slightly diminished . . .
>
> *Spy,* June 1988

Here is a more elaborate example of a roundup lead. If you read it carefully you'll see that it contains a central weakness. What, in your opinion, is that weakness?

> I { Three of the television stations owned by the Washington Post Company refuse to carry a series of Mobil Oil Corp. commercials, declaring that the spots are a form of unacceptable "editorial advertising" that they are entitled to reject. The ads, cast in the form of animal fables, artfully argue company opposition to Government regulation and to windfall profits taxes.

II ｜ A few days later, the stations owned by ABC, CBS and NBC turn down another Mobil spot that attempts to put oil company profits "in perspective" by arguing that Mobil's earnings as a percentage of money invested were less than for . . . guess who? . . . ABC, CBS and NBC.

III ｜ CBS's Ray Brady, on the *CBS Evening News*, describes how oil companies can use creative bookkeeping to make it seem as if certain of their profits are coming from abroad rather than from the American consumer. Brady does his "standupper" analysis in front of a Mobil gas station sign, on the day that Mobil releases its third-quarter figures. Mobil, saying it doesn't use such scams, accuses CBS of playing "fast and loose with the truth."

GENERAL STATEMENT ｜ Even a casual watcher of television over the last few months would have picked up on the news that a red-hot war seems to be going on between the major oil companies and the major television companies.

TV Guide, May 17–23, 1980

So, what's the structural flaw in this roundup lead?

Put simply, it lacks diversity. The story is: War between the media and major oil companies. Yet only one oil company is cited in all three examples.

THE INDIRECT LEAD

This kind of lead seeks to arouse the curiosity of the reader by approaching the point of the article in a roundabout fashion. It may tell a little story, describe a place, or relate a little bit of history. The reader asks: Why am I being taken on this ramble through irrelevancy? Then, suddenly, the indirect lead turns a corner and loops into the main theme of the article. The forms of the indirect lead are so flexible and so diverse that, like the charms of Cleopatra, age cannot wither nor custom stale their infinite variety. For this reason they are hard to classify. But from the wealth of possibility there emerge three basic types:

1. Anecdotal, plus general statement
2. Scene-setter, plus general statement
3. Recap, plus general statement

The Anecdote

The anecdotal lead tells a short, pointed story about a situation. Sometimes this story is merely typical of an individual's life, or of a broad social condition. And sometimes it simply plunges the reader into a specific predicament. Here is an example of the latter:

> One hundred seven stories high over Manhattan, a group of diners at the World Trade Center's skyscraping restaurant Windows on the World downed their digestifs, took a last glance at the stunning light show below, and crowded into a waiting down elevator. The doors slid shut. The elevator didn't budge. Someone stabbed irritably at the button. Nothing happened. Somebody else got the doors open and the passengers free. "The elevator's out," one of them huffily informed a white-jacketed captain. The captain shrugged toward the lightscape outside, gone suddenly inky black. "So's New York," he replied. . . .
>
> GENERAL STATEMENT { On a muggy dog-day evening last week, a vagrant summer storm knocked out high-voltage power lines in the near New York exurbs — and within an hour returned 9 million people to the dark, heat and disquiet of a pre-electric age.
>
> *Newsweek*, July 25, 1977

Alternatively, an opening anecdote can be a highly effective way of getting a reader into a personality profile. The incident, however, cannot be just any happening in the subject's life; it must exemplify the psychological quirk or characteristic that makes that individual interesting, that justifies a major magazine article about that person. The selection of such an incident requires considerable insight. Indeed, it often requires writers to do mini-psychoanalyses of their subjects. What makes them tick? Why are they of interest to the reader? Here is an example:

> One freezing morning last December, Sen. William Proxmire of Wisconsin joined a New York City sanitation crew and spent half a day wrestling garbage cans along a route in Brooklyn. What impelled the 62-year-old Senator to undertake such a chore? Very simple, says Proxmire. As chairman of the Senate banking committee, he had oversight responsibilities for New York's federal loan program and thus was interested in the efficiency of the city's operations. There was no better way to study sanitation than to join a garbage crew . . .
>
> GENERAL STATEMENT { The incident typifies Proxmire's offbeat approach to his job. He is a legendary eccentric and a superb self-promoter . . .
>
> *Reader's Digest*, November 1978

The element of paradox is clear in this lead. What, the reader asks, is a distinguished senator doing hauling garbage? We are quickly told the ostensible reason — Proxmire is curious — but this answer merely leaves us with a more profound question: What kind of a man would do such a thing? Before we know it, we are deep into the profile.

The Scene-setter

This kind of lead shares many characteristics in common with the anecdotal lead. But instead of telling a story, it describes a scene, or puts a character in a setting that sets the story in motion. Here is an example:

> Christmas morning in the presidential residence, a white stucco mansion on the banks of the Nile, Jihan el-Sadat is seated upon a silken sofa, her Brussels griffon lapdog, Beauty, beside her. Sunlight streams through the high windows into the antique-filled room, lighting up the wall tapestry with its hunting scene. Oriental rugs are set upon gleaming hardwood floors beneath crystal chandeliers . . .

GENERAL STATEMENT { Jihan Sadat is also — by conviction and by reason of her relationship to the man who runs the nation — Egypt's leading feminist.

New York Times Magazine, March 16, 1980

Here is another example:

> Riding high above the freeway, nestled in pleated burgundy leather, we barrel across Colorado in our "purty Peterbilt," with Al Jarreau serenading us on the truck's radio. As Tim and I head west toward Denver, the Rockies appear in the distance and instantly begin to rise, back-lit by the setting sun. It's one of those magical moments when, after a hard day of driving, I feel the power and the freedom, the sense of adventure that taking the wheel of a fancy truck has come to symbolize. A year earlier, I wouldn't have given the world of trucks a thought, except to grumble when one of the monsters whizzed by me on the highway. Now, sitting behind the wheel, I am part of the myth.

GENERAL STATEMENT { My transformation to lady truck driver began the day I met Tim. I'd spent my working life in retailing, as a model at Bergdorf's in New York, then . . .

Cosmopolitan, June 1982

The element of paradox is clear in the second example. We are thrust into the scene, roaring down the highway in a huge vehicle traditionally piloted by males of the strongest *machismo* — only to find a woman at the wheel. In the first example the regal scene is majestically set and the contradiction is more implied than actual when we hear that the elegant Mrs. Sadat, before the assassination of her husband, was leading a very tough revolution — far tougher than any on this side of the Atlantic — for the rights of her country's women.

Both anecdotal and scene-setter leads attempt to intrigue the reader by a process of colorful indirection. We wonder why we are given minute details of the final seconds of a dinner 107 stories over Manhattan; we are perplexed by the idea of a senator slinging garbage; we are curious about the woman roaring along the highway in the cab of an 18-wheeler.

The Recap

The recap lead also intrigues by indirection, but it is a different kind of indirection. It generally recapitulates a historical situation fairly well known to the readership; then, just when the readers are beginning to wonder why the article bothers to go through all this dusty background, a new twist is introduced that forms the major theme of the piece. The lead on Aristotle at the beginning of this chapter is an example of a recap lead. We all know Aristotle was a fusty old grind, and he had to be born somewhere in Greece. Our interest is just beginning to peel off when suddenly we are told this paragon made some awesome mistakes. Here is another example:

> Centuries ago, the Roman poet Martial recognized that parents could inflict psychological and economic hardship on their children by disinheriting them. "If you want them to mourn," he dryly noted, "you had best leave them nothing." Two thousand years later, people still follow his advice and vindictively leave their children little but a
> GENERAL { legacy of infighting and guilt. Yet other, more benign, motives seem
> STATEMENT { to be multiplying.
>
> *Psychology Today*, May 1980

Of course, not all recap leads need to have classical overtones. Often the affairs in question go back no more than a few days or weeks. The news magazines are particularly fond of this kind of lead because it enables them to summarize events in a fast, colorful fashion and then dive into some new development. Here are two examples.

> When Leslie Manigat came to power in Haiti in January, the best that could be said of the long-exiled professor of political science was that

he represented a slight improvement over the 30 years of Duvalier dictatorship and the two years of military rule that followed. True, the elections had been rigged. True, the military still loomed large in affairs. Yet the portly, smiling 57-year-old President in a white suit *was* a civilian — and that gave some Haitians a modicum of hope that a first step toward democracy had been taken. Last week, such hopes sank as low as Haiti's gross national product as Lt. Gen. Henri Namphy, the strong man who engineered the election of Manigat, ousted him in a bloodless coup and packed him off to a new exile in the Dominican Republic next door.

GENERAL
STATEMENT

U.S. News & World Report, July 4, 1988

America, the great receiver. From every culture to arrive within its borders, it embraces some new ingredient. Puritan wrath. Black cool. Irish poetics. Jewish irony. One after another, America draws them down the channels of its awareness and puts them into play in new settings. They collide and cross-pollinate and mix it up, nowhere more so than in the arts and popular culture. Sparks fly at the meeting points. The Jewish novel works variations on the keynotes of Puritan gloom. The western is re-seen through John Ford's Irish eyes. Sinatra meets Duke Ellington. Every offering is admitted and set dancing with new partners. It may be better to give, but it's a lot more fun to receive.

GENERAL
STATEMENT

Nowadays the mainstream is receiving a rich new current. More and more, American film, theater, music, design, dance and art are taking on a Hispanic color and spirit. Look around.

Time, July 11, 1988

In this chapter we have examined a wide range of leads, and made some analysis of why each is effective as a way of getting into a story. In each case I have taken care to connect the lead with a general statement, which should always be viewed as an integral part of the introductory material. A lead, no matter how well crafted, cannot thrive in a vacuum, it must be cemented into the idea of the article's main theme.

ASSIGNMENT

Reread the material on microamp medicine outlined at the end of chapter 3 and attempt to fashion from it realistic examples of the three major kinds of lead:

1. Startling assertion
2. Roundup or bullet
3. Indirect

If you have the time, attempt to devise examples of the three basic kinds of indirect lead — anecdotal, scene-setter, and recap. Take care to ensure that all the sample leads connect directly into a general statement that embraces the main theme of the article.

Example Solutions

1. *Startling assertion*

GENERAL STATEMENT

We hear much about the cures of miracle drugs — and quite a bit about their chilling side effects — but today the most miraculous cures of all are achieved by a new branch of medicine that uses no drugs at all. By transmitting minute pulses of electricity through afflicted tissues, doctors are now able to heal everything from spine curvature and epilepsy to bedsores and broken bones that refuse to knit back together. The effectiveness of electromedicine was first discovered . . .

2. *Roundup (or Bullet)*

In New York a twenty-six-year old man suffering from uncontrollable daily epileptic seizure is, after a small operation, able to lead a normal life.

In Toronto a child with a spinal curvature so acute she had to spend most of her day curled up on a hospital pallet is now able to join her friends in all but the roughest playground games.

In Paris, the Necker Hospital has perfected a new way to send wounded soldiers to sleep without suffering possible adverse effects of drugs.

GENERAL STATEMENT

In every instance the medical breakthrough is owing to a new branch of the healing arts known as electromedicine. By transmitting small pulses of electric current . . .

3. *Indirect*

ANECDOTE

Dr. Michael Bobech, an expert on human muscle disorders, was working in his lab one day late in 1971 in an experiment on a pig afflicted with an 18-degree spinal curvature. Previous research had revealed that muscle spasms can be both induced and eliminated by the application of minute impulses of electrical energy. Perhaps, Bobech reasoned, spinal curvature, or scoliosis — the seemingly incurable ailment afflicting thousands of newborn children every year — could be viewed simply as a prolonged muscle spasm and treated accordingly. The doctor proceeded to place some small electrodes in the taut muscles along the pig's back and pass small electric pulses through them.

To Bobech's surprise, the pig's spinal curvature was quickly halved, and soon eliminated. He applied the same technique to scoliotic children with the same result; the doctor had, by the application of a new healing procedure now known as electromedicine, shown that one of the most crippling of childhood afflictions was no longer incurable.

GENERAL
STATEMENT

Since then electromedicine, developed in research centers in New York, Paris, Seattle, and Toronto, has shown itself capable of healing such ailments as . . .

SCENE-SETTER

Beth Ganz, the eight-year-old daughter of a Toronto accountant, shouts and dances in the school playground now. In a while she will ride her yellow bike home and invite some friends to eat a few of the chocolate chip cookies she baked herself.

GENERAL
STATEMENT

Life was not always so easy for Beth. Until last year a crippling 38-degree curvature of the spine forced her to spend eighteen hours a day curled up on a cot, being fed by her mother. But thanks to the development of a new branch of science known as electromedicine, she can enjoy the life . . .

RECAP

For the first seven years of her life Beth Ganz, eight, was afflicted with a 38-degree spinal curvature. So acute was her condition that she had to be fed by her mother and spend up to 18 hours a day curled up on a hospital bed. Yet today, after undergoing a new kind of treatment devised by Dr. Michael Bobech of Toronto, Canada, Beth can feed herself, ride a bike, bake cookies, and attend school with her friends.

GENERAL
STATEMENT

"This treatment has transformed Beth from a vegetable to a lively, active school girl," declares her father, a Toronto accountant. The treatment is just one instance of a new mode of healing generally known as electromedicine. It can also cure . . .

STORY ORGANIZATION 1
The Personality Profile . . .
Warts and All

ROBERT RUARK (1915–1965) was one of this century's most prolific and best-paid journalists. Besides selling some 1,500 articles to magazines, he wrote a syndicated newspaper column and half a dozen best-selling books (including *Uhuru, Something of Value,* and *The Old Man and the Boy*). He was acquainted with many fashionable screen beauties and with such men as Bernard Baruch, Franklin Roosevelt, and Winston Churchill. Ruark regularly made more than a quarter of a million dollars a year with his typewriter. And he was seldom at a loss for ideas. On one occasion, anxious to leave for a safari in Africa, he rented a hotel room and hammered out sixteen impeccably crafted newspaper columns in the space of a single day.

A few months before his death by bottle, Ruark sat drinking with an old friend, Bill Roberts, in a corner booth at Houston's plush International Club. Roberts, who was then a columnist with the *Houston Post,* had asked Ruark a question: How do you write a magazine article? Ruark pulled a piece of copy paper from his pocket and signaled one of the green-jacketed waiters for another round of martinis.

"Simple," he said, and began to trace a series of hen scratches on the copy paper. A personality profile, he declared, should be organized in the pattern of this sketch, with the appearance of a tin man (see fig. 5).

"It's what all the editors want, Willie," he told Roberts, "especially if they don't know you. I could start off with my laundry list now, and sell the piece. But the classic is this."

Ruark then proceeded to illustrate his point by taking the story of his own life, laced with a strong dash of Walter Mitty. For his lead

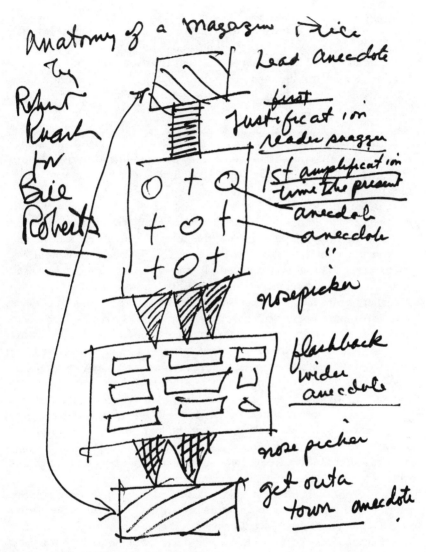

Fig. 5. Robert Ruark's tinman diagram.

Ruark selected an incident from his youth in which he fought off a wild-cat with his bare hands. Far more than his friendships with the mighty and his journalistic triumphs, he felt that this incident put on display the real Ruark. By now the reader is curious. How can a fourteen-year-old boy grapple with an angry wildcat and come out on top? There is a clear element of paradox, and the reader is ripe for the section named Justification, in which he is told of three additional achievements by the subject. Here Ruark cites the "facts" that (1) he owns fourteen Rolls Royces, (2) has fifteen mistresses, and (3) writes a column syndicated to 2 million newspapers. By now the reader is asking: How is this possible? and we are ready to plunge into the next section, called Amplification.

This catechism of question and response, justly done, is one of the central skills of any person who would write for or edit magazines. The answer to each question — and it must be a genuine answer — is subtly structured to lure the reader ever deeper into the subject matter of the story.

Amplification, for Ruark, is made up of an account of the subject's present-day doings and achievements: the appearance of a new book, the flat in London's Mayfair district, the hunting lodge in Africa, the villa in Spain, the contract for a new movie script. This section is relatively easy to write. But there is a problem. It may become so upbeat, so bushy-tailed that the story begins to lose credibility. Nobody can be *that* good, the readers begin to say to themselves. To allay this growing skepticism Ruark introduces a new element that he terms the "Nosepicker" or, to employ the word used by many magazine editors, the "Wart."* This consists of an incident or anecdote that, in Ruark's words, "reflects discredit, in a nice way, on the subject." Sometimes, if the subject has been very naughty, the Wart may not be presented in such a nice way. In Ruark's profile the incident might concern his heavy drinking, someone wrongfully abused in his column, or the treatment of Virginia, his wife of twenty-four years.

Encouraged by the thought that the hero, too, has human flaws, the reader formulates a new question: How did this person get this way? It is a question that leads him into Flashback, or History. For Ruark this includes a touching account of growing up dirt poor in North Carolina, a virtual orphan. The theme builds through lesser journalistic achievements, World War II, and so on to the present day. Lest the subject begin to walk upon water again, Ruark specifies that it is now time for another Wart. Perhaps it will concern his ill-informed condemnation of the Peace Corps, or some observations he was once tempted to make about the sanctity of motherhood.

By now the readers have heard about the subject's present life and

---

*The word *wart* is derived from the instructions Oliver Cromwell gave to the man painting his picture. "Remark," said the blunt English dictator, "all these roughnesses, pimples, warts and everything as you see me, otherwise I will never pay a farthing for it."

his past life. All we are left to wonder about is his future. Or, in the short-hand of the trade, Whither Ruark? New scripts, new projects, new doctors, new marriages? Most of Ruark's published magazine profiles contain at least a brief section on where the subject is going from here. But for some reason Ruark has not included this segment on his diagram. Perhaps the dry martinis were exacting their toll that day in Houston. Or perhaps Ruark knew, even then, that he had but a few months to live.

With the future sketched in, it only remains for the writer to seal off the entire article with a closing anecdote, termed a "Get Outa Town." Ruark suggests that this peroration should help make the piece into a dramatically rounded whole by establishing a certain resonance with the opening anecdote. For this reason Ruark closes with an encounter the middle-aged journalist had with an African leopard. This contrived resonance with the lead, this repeated idea of a man grappling wild beasts with his bare hands is brought home by the long arrow running up the left-hand side of Ruark's diagram.

THE LEAD

There is a clear line of logic in the Ruark system. If you doubt this then try rearranging the material in a different order, and see how it looks. Can we really talk about a person's past before we know who he or she is? Does it make sense to speak of that person's future before we have cast back into his or her early years?

In the previous chapter we noted that though there is a great variety of leads, there is an obvious reason for opening a personality profile with an anecdote about the subject. That anecdote cannot be just any incident involving that person; it must somehow typify the essential core of his or her individuality. More, it must also highlight the aspect of the personality most likely to appeal to the readers. In a sense, the selection of such an anecdote requires the writer (or editor) to perform a mini-psychoanalysis of both subject and readership. What qualities make the subject stand out from his or her fellow human beings? What aspects of his or her personality make the person of special interest to the readers? The readers of *People* want to hear about movie star Desiree Pinhead's amours, and her spats in the studio. The readers of *Weight Watchers* want to know about the techniques she used to lose fifty pounds in five weeks.

Because it involves psychoanalysis — both of subject and reader-ship — the business of choosing the right opening anecdote is never simple.

We used to set magazine students at Syracuse University an assignment on the late Steve McQueen. Students were given a jumble of facts on Mc-Queen and asked to build them into a coherent profile. The material itself was exciting because McQueen, unlike many stars, led a life that resembled that of the characters he played. Among his real-life adventures McQueen grew up in a California reform school, forged some seaman's papers to escape aboard a tanker, and jumped ship in the Dominican Republic. He was a bartender in a Texas brothel before joining the Marines at the age of seventeen. While in the service he was demoted seven times for insubordination. McQueen subsequently owned and raced his own car at Sebring and performed his own motorbike stunts in the movie *The Great Escape*. Plenty of fine material, but where to start? Which incident really sums up the essence of this Hollywood success who refused to take crap from anybody?

How about an opener on the racetrack at Sebring? Or in the midst of a stunt? The students tried everything. The Marines? The brothel? Many of the leads were quite effective, but one stood out. The student described McQueen during lunch break on the set of his latest movie. Most of the cast sat at a trestle table, eating off china plates. In contrast, McQueen was seated nearby on a pile of lumber, a sandwich in one hand and his dessert, a slice of apple pie, in the other. That tightly clasped slice of pie said it all. What better way to show the reader the essence of a man who, for all his success, had had his character molded in the dog-eat-dog setting of a reform school for boys?

Such subtle psychological insights are central to the business of creating an effective personality profile. Many magazine writers get so close to their material that they cannot distill the defining qualities of their subject. Or, perhaps, they are shaky about the identity of the readers. In these cases it is often the task of the editor, with his or her broader perspective, to read the rough draft through and say to the writer: "Hey, your lead's in the seventh paragraph."

JUSTIFICATION

The key to writing an effective justification in a profile is to take an idea imparted by an opening anecdote, sum it up in a general statement of theme, and then embellish it with three (or maybe four) disparate achievements of the subject. This diversity is important, for it presents the reader with a sense of dramatic tension so that he or she is compelled to ask: How is this possible?

These achievements should on no account be deducible, one from another. Robert Ruark used (1) fourteen Rolls Royces (suggesting wealth), (2) fifteen mistresses (a kind of tacky charm), and (3) a column running in 2 million newspapers (a form of literacy). These qualities cannot be deduced, one from another. Great wealth does not imply charm, any more than charm implies literacy. Nor does literacy imply wealth. There is a dramatic tension among these three kinds of achievement, an element of paradox, of seeming contradiction that lures the readers in and compels them to ask: How can these qualities coexist in one person? The reader answers this question by plunging into the body of the story.

Diversity is the essence of justification. Yet beginners sometimes have difficulty grasping this. All too often they select a subject's achievements from a single dimension of his or her personality. Let us assume you have been assigned to write a profile of John F. Kennedy. In your justification you could describe him as a U.S. president, a senator, and before that a congressman from Massachusetts. How predictable—and how boring! All three points stand in a line, as depicted in figure 6, *a*. How much more interesting to describe Kennedy as a Navy war hero, the author of a Pulitzer prize-winning book on American history, and the romancer of Mafia-connected women. Unless you hold a particularly perverse view of the universe, none of these accomplishments is readily deducible from the other. The dramatic tension is clear. The points, if you like, stand in a triangle, as depicted in figure 6, *b*. They are trying to fly apart, and it

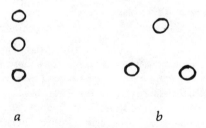

a   *b*

Fig. 6. Justification, good and bad.

is only the human being in which they coexist that holds them together. One is curious about such a being, so the final diagram of a well-constructed justification might come to look like the diagram in figure 7.

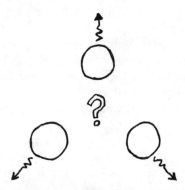

Fig. 7. Justification: creating a point of curiosity.

Here is an example of this mode of presentation from *Newsweek*'s cover story on entrepreneur-sportsman Ted Turner. The story opens like this:

> As usual Ted Turner couldn't wait to start talking. Minutes before the camera's ruby light flashed on, cable TV's garrulous impresario was already well into his inaugural address before a gathering of Atlanta VIPs. By the time he actually went on the air, Turner was proudly reciting from an ode to himself composed by his public relations man ("To act upon one's convictions while others wait/To create a positive force in a world where cynics abound . . ."). At last, he proclaimed: "I dedicate this news channel for America." Drums rolled, flags ascended and three military bands blared the national anthem. As the last notes faded, Turner whooped out a lusty "Awwriiight!" With that, he thrust into motion a historic television breakthrough — the world's first 24-hour-a-day network devoted entirely to news.

GENERAL
STATEMENT

JUSTIFI-
CATION,
1, 2, and 3

> The Cable News Network (CNN), which arrived in 2.2 million homes last week, is the latest and most audacious venture of one of today's most intriguing entrepreneurs. Flamboyant owner of Atlanta's major-league baseball and basketball teams, swashbuckling winner of the last America's Cup yachting series, and operator of the first nationally televised "superstation," 41-year-old Robert Edward Turner III has so incensed, perplexed and dazzled his many adversaries that he has become something of a Southern folk hero. Now he is about . . .
>
> *Newsweek*, June 16, 1980

We have here a scene-setter anecdotal lead, followed by a general statement (intriguing entrepreneur) that points up what that leading anecdote means, and three disparate points of justification. Turner is the owner of ball clubs, a hands-on racing skipper, and the operator of a new kind of television network. None of these achievements is readily derivable from the others, and the readers may wonder: How is all this possible in one man? The reader is now poised to enter the next segment of the story.

AMPLIFICATION

The most challenging and time-consuming aspect of editing any personality profile is undoubtedly the selection and arrangement of material for the lead and justification. One-third, or even one-half, of an editor's time may be devoted to the task of getting these opening paragraphs straight. They form the foundation of the story. If the material is sloppily arranged, the story will collapse like a house of cards. If it is well presented, the reader will be eager to accept the more discursive elaboration of amplification. The pressure, in a sense, is off. The "sale" is made and the reader is now seated and ready to absorb everything the writer has to say. The tone is conversational. The subject matter will contain numerous anecdotes and quotations, and may fill as much as one-half or more of the total story space.

WARTS

The editorial function of the "wart" is both complicated and important. By mentioning the subject's shortcomings, the writer is clearly demonstrating his or her objectivity and thus, somewhat backhandedly, enhancing the credibility of the profile's more complimentary material. If we hear that Turner bawls out his ball players when they lose, we are more likely to believe the magazine when it tells us he is kind to his wife. But the wart has another important function. Paragons of virtue are always boring. The ancient Greeks knew this; the doings of their gods and goddesses intrigue today not because of their great strengths, but because those strengths were coupled with terrible weaknesses. Aphrodite, the goddess of love, repeatedly attempted to murder Psyche for falling in love with her son. And great Zeus himself took the liberty of marrying his sister Hera and usurping his own father from his position as the lord of creation.

The wart, be it in Greek myth or a modern personality profile, makes the subject plausible. It invites the reader to judge, and compare the subject's life to their own lives. We do not have Ruark's talents, but then neither do we have his problem with liquor and women. We do not plot the murder of the woman who loves our son. Nor do we throw our father out of his palace. By inviting this adverse comparison, the writer is both drawing the reader deeper into the story and giving him or her a harmless little fillip of superiority over the subject.

In many personality profiles the wart material is obvious. It generally takes the form of an anecdote, a short story about an event or a decision of which the subject is not proud. But, like lead anecdotes, such stories must be keyed. The reader must be informed of their point. Here is an example from the Ted Turner story in *Newsweek:*

> "If you live in Kansas, do you really care about the comings and goings of ministers at a conference in Luxembourg?"

SIGNPOSTS {Such skepticism carries over to Turner's credentials as a broadcast journalism reformer. Until recently, his WTBS superstation featured a morning newscast in which anchor man Bill Tush, with Turner's approval, indulged in such stunts as superimposing a picture of Walter Cronkite over his head and bringing on a German shepherd, outfit-

WARTS {ted with shirt and tie, as his guest co-anchor. Whenever things got dull, Tush would start tossing around lemon-meringue pies. Although Turner has since . . .

If the editor just dropped the incidents of Cronkite's photo, the pies, and the anchor dog into the copy after the Luxembourg quote, the reader would have no understanding of their point. Yet, time and again aspiring editors do just this, leaving their audience to speculate about what it all means. Does it mean Turner is a fun guy? Does it mean he has a warped admiration for Soupy Sales? Or what?

I suspect this reluctance to signpost a reader into adverse material stems from the editor's careful schooling in objectivity. Let the facts speak for themselves. To write that "Such skepticism carries over to Turner's credentials as a broadcast journalism reformer" seems unfair. It seems to load the dice. Yet it is impossible to signpost a wart without incurring some element of judgment, even if it is simply pointing out that the subject's behavior is abnormal. So the judgment must be made. But it must also be firmly supported by the following material.

The subjects of most profiles are active, successful people, and in their climb to the top some aspect of their lives has become distorted. Perhaps there is a cruel divorce, neglected children, or a broken deal that signifies the price they paid on the climb upward. But there will always be some individuals who make the ascent without putting a foot wrong.

There are no warts. The writer and editor cannot lay a glove on them. And yet, there is always *something*, even if it has to be derived from the subject's special strengths. Perhaps Walter Hoving, the retired chairman of Tiffany, is just such a straight arrow. A successful businessman, possessed of impeccable taste, Hoving is a religious man who insists on the highest ethical standards for himself and those he employs. Here's how *New York* magazine laid its wart upon him:

> "Walter Hoving has been larger than life," says Ralph Destino, president of Cartier Inc. "All New York will miss him."
>
> There are some others, however, who will heave a sigh of relief at Hoving's departure, for he has never felt the slightest hesitation at inflicting his highly subjective views on everything from "vulgar" Christmas decorations to the dangers of buying diamonds and gold bars.
>
> *New York*, December 22, 1980

FLASHBACK

In a sense, the flashback part of a profile is the easiest to write. It is composed of what E. M. Forster, in his classic work *Aspects of the Novel*, termed a simple narration of "and then . . . and then." One begins with the subject's birth and earliest years and moves forward in a chronicle of events that culminates in present times. In fact, this narration is so easy to assemble that many inexperienced writers are tempted to lunge at it prematurely. A snappy lead then bingo, Ted Turner, born in 1939. . . . The writer, and the editor, must of course resist this temptation, for the reader has yet to be sold on the importance of the subject.

As flashback comes to a close, it is likely that the subject is beginning to walk on water again and it becomes necessary to administer another wart. The structure of wart II resembles that of wart I. But, like the diverse achievements of justification, the two shortcomings should not be closely related to each other.

WHITHER?

The third major section of the profile is also relatively easy to write and to organize. Its chief problem is, simply, that many writers forget it, as did Ruark in his diagram. All it takes is a question toward the end of the interview: "Mr. Turner, what do you intend to do when you have completed these projects? What plans do you have for the future?" In response, the subject will probably talk for half an hour. These revelations often form the most interesting part of the interview, in the same way that a person's hopes are always more revealing than his or her accomplishments. Yet these are the questions that so many reporters fail to ask; in the long run perhaps this omission is a boon for editors, for it lets them call up the important personage themselves and say, "Hey, what's next?"

GET OUTA TOWN

Like the lead, this should be an anecdote or incident that brings out the essential quality of the subject. In many ways it may resemble the lead, and set up a distinctive resonance with it that brings the intervening material into focus. Selecting such an anecdote is not always easy, and I have heard writers say, "I've got a great lead, but nothing for the kicker." If there is clearly no available material, then it can only be for one of two reasons. Either the writer has not done sufficient research, or the opening anecdote does not hook into one of the subject's central traits. Conversely, if the lead derives four-square from the center of the subject's personality, then there is bound to be a wealth of affiliated anecdotes for "getting outa town." Here's how the writer of the Turner profile pulled it all together:

> As for CNN's chances for survival, the fact that it is Ted Turner's current crusade may be reason enough to anticipate success. George Babick, head of CNN's New York sales office, offers perhaps the wisest advice about how to regard anything his boss touches: "If Ted predicted the sun will come up in the west tomorrow morning, you'd laugh and say he's full of it. But you'd still set the alarm. You wouldn't want to miss the miracle."

> Turner's latest "miracle" rose last week. It will be worth watching.
> *Newsweek*, June 16, 1980

The profile opened with a scene-setter of Turner's unorthodox promotional speech for CNN, and now the writer brings us full circle by speculating on the new network's chances, and closes with a wryly upbeat evaluation of Turner's promotional ability.

Some readers will undoubtedly feel that Ruark's diagram for the organization of the personality profile is too structured and too dogmatic.

Why, they may wonder, should I force my material into this ironclad mold? Facts, surely, have a vitality of their own, and it is that vitality that should determine the structure of my story.

Robert Ruark, were he alive today, might take another sip of vodka martini and bare his teeth in a competitive grin. When you can sell an interview with your laundry list, he might say, then you can knead and warp the organizational forms into any shape you choose. In the meantime, however, Ruark's advice to Bill Roberts holds true: "It's what all the editors want, Willie, especially if they don't know you."

ASSIGNMENT

Read the following personality profile from the *Reader's Digest* on Robin Williams and analyze it in terms of the Ruark diagram, indicating in the margin what you think is the lead, general statement, justification, amplification, wart I, flashback, wart II, whither, and GOT. Where does the organization of the Williams piece differ from that of Ruark, as outlined in this chapter? Are any sections omitted? Would the Williams piece be strengthened if it were rearranged? Hints: Take a close look at the lead; is it the best opening available? Could the general statement be refocused? Be prepared to penetrate deep cover in search of warts. Does all the stuff in the box belong there? Good luck.

THE ZANY WORLD OF ROBIN WILLIAMS

By John Culhane

Yesterday's Mork is today's virtuoso of improvisational, freewheeling comedy, forever game to spin off at warp speed into the wild ad-lib yonder

When Robin Williams's son Zachary, was two years old, his parents went out for an evening, leaving him with a baby-sitter. As Williams pulled away in his car, he looked back and saw his son's tear-streaked face at the window.

A year later, on a 23-city tour of the United States, Williams stood on the stage of the Metropolitan Opera House in New York City and talked about that moment.

"As you walked out of the house," said Robin, "the last thing you saw was a little face pressed up against the window, going. . . ." Robin raised his hands above his ears and splayed his fingers as if they were pressed against plate glass, contorting his mouth as if he were a baby screaming, but of course you couldn't hear through the "window." Parents throughout the audience burst out laughing in the shock of recognition. The comedian had captured in pantomime the quintessential crying kid.

Coming up consistently with the unexpected yet exactly right line or facial expression has made Robin Williams, at age 36, the top banana in the bunch of funnymen who have revived live stand-up comedy in America. Through his voice, postures and gestures, people end up in the most unlikely and absurd situations. He is William F. Buckley, Jr., host of TV's "Firing Line," discussing the social ramifications of "Goldilocks and the Three Bears"; he is a woman confusing the can of Mace in her handbag with a breath freshener; he is Mister Rogers as a future President. ("Can *you* say Armageddon? . . . I think it's too late.") His imagination moves at warp speed. He is Robin unHoodwinked, aiming his arrows at dependence on drugs, politicians, television, at a world that devotes major energies to blowing itself up. "The Iran-Iraq War, Middle East Side Story," he says. "Iran . . . and we sold them missiles; now they fire missiles back at us — carrying little signs that say, 'Isn't it ironic?' BAM!"

Robinwacky. Most people became aware of Robin Williams's peculiar gifts through his portrayal of an alien trying to cope with American society on the television series "Mork & Mindy" (1978–1982). There followed several films, including the title role in *The World According to Garp*, from John Irving's best-selling novel, and *Moscow on the Hudson*, in which Williams played a Russian defector.

His latest film, *Good Morning, Vietnam*, is the first to take full advantage of his supersonic flights of improvisational comedy. The story is based on the life of airman Adrian Cronauer, a disc jockey who broadcast for the Armed Forces Radio Service in Saigon in 1965. Director Barry Levinson had Williams do some broadcasts as written on the first take, but permitted him to soar off on subsequent takes into the wild ad-lib yonder. The finished "broadcasts" are almost all pure, unscripted Williams.   4

For sustained Robinwacky, fans can enjoy his concert performances on three record albums and three videocassettes. Then there are his numerous TV appearances, including "Comic Relief," cable-television benefits he helped organize that have brought in over $5 million for the nation's homeless. Cable television also broadcast his one-man show at the Metropolitan Opera, which featured comic essays on sex, love, marriage and parenting, as well as his rendition of Elmer Fudd singing Wagner's "Ride of the Valkyries." Small wonder that *Newsweek* described his attraction as "the spectacle of a brain on constant spin cycle."

Coming-Out Party. Robin Williams   1 was the only child of the second marriages of both his parents. His father, Robert Williams, was a Ford Motor Company executive, and Robin was raised in the affluent suburbs of Lake Forest, outside Chicago, and Bloomfield Hills, near Detroit.

He got his basic idea of comedy from his mother, Laurie. "Comedy was a kind of communication for my mother and me. She told funny jokes that kind of embarrassed my father but made me laugh."

As a child he preferred to play alone, creating his own world with toy soldiers. He loved books, cartoons on TV, and comedian Jonathan Winters on "The Jack Paar Show." Delighted by Winters's amazing aptitude for improvisation and mimicry, Robin would eventually adopt the same stream-of-consciousness comedy style.

Williams remembers himself in the

eighth grade as "short, squat and picked on." But unlike other youngsters who developed comedy as a defense, Robin took up wrestling and cross-country running. "I was not a class cut-up at all," he says. "I was very straight. Future accountants of America."

In his senior year, his family moved to Marin county, outside San Francisco, where Robin acted in his first school play. "I played a crazy character and I got laughs," he says. He didn't realize, though, that there was a comedian inside him trying to get out.

"I didn't come out of myself until the first year of college," he recalls. "Then I kind of exploded."

The fuse was lighted by his love of different languages. Thinking he might like to be a foreign-service officer, he enrolled as a freshman at Claremont Men's College near Los Angeles and studied political science and economics. He also took a course in improv-isation (because he found the teacher attractive) and discovered that the class laughed at his spontaneous remarks.

"That was the trigger event," he says, looking back, "because it was so easy for me. It was instantaneous. It also seemed mine."

But the example of his father, who died last year, was what freed him to go into comedy. "My father gave up a lot of money to live happily. He left Ford and went to live in a tiny house in Tiburon, Calif., to be near the ocean and not be at the whims of people. That said to me, 'If you find something you want to do, do it.'"

Tower of Babel. Robin left Claremont and went to the College of Marin to study acting. Then he heard that Juilliard in New York had set up an acting school. Robin auditioned, won a scholarship and arrived there in the fall of 1973.

The Many Voices of Robin Williams

A full listing of all the voices that live inside Robin Williams would probably fill a small-town phone book. Here is some directory assistance:

Roosevelt E. Roosevelt, an uncooperative weatherman: "You got a window? Open it."

A black female sex therapist named Dr. Roof: "Get yoh act together, now. Yoh look lahk a Ken doll."

A baby in his mother's womb: "It sure is nice — except when she dances."

A restaurant critic: "Here's a little advice: don't eat at a restaurant located next to a pound."

Mr. Leo, fashion designer in Vietnam: "Today I'd like to talk about the enemy, and what they're wearing. They're wearing black. I say you can fight in the jungle in it, and at night put on some pearls and you're ready for formal wear. They're dressed in pajamas. It's casual. It says, 'I can fight or I can just lay around.'"

His child at 35 (happy dream): "I'd like to thank the Nobel Academy."

His child at 35 (bad dream): "You want fries with this?"

His elocution teacher, misreading his potential, criticized him by saying, "You're mimicking people. Where is *your* voice?" For three years he sought his own style, while acting in plays by authors ranging from Shakespeare to Ibsen. (In his Emmy-winning performance on a Carol Burnett special in 1987, he became Shakespeare, improvising in iambic pentameter.)

Williams left Juilliard after three years, without graduating, to be with his girlfriend in San Francisco. He worked days at an ice-cream parlor and at night took classes in comedy. Once, when Robin did an improvisation, the audience broke up. It reminded him of his Claremont class. "It was the same rush—like when a football player breaks through the line and sees open field in front of him." Soon he was doing stand-up improvisational comedy in small clubs.

In 1978 the creators of TV's "Happy Days" auditioned him for the role of an alien from outer space. Asked to sit down as an alien would, Williams jumped on a chair and stood on his head. The part was his.

Mail response to the episode was so enthusiastic that "Mork & Mindy" went on the air without a pilot, became an instant hit and made "Na-no-Na-no" (an alien's way of saying "hello" and "good-by") the nation's favorite catch phrase.

Robin Williams had found his voice, which turned out to be a modern Tower of Babel. He could speak with the tongues of men, angels, animals, vegetables and minerals. When he played Vladimir Ivanoff in *Moscow on the Hudson*, Vincent Canby of the New York *Times* called his performance "extraordinarily complex . . . his Russian sounds amazingly, comically authentic."

Much of his early success, however, was marred by a growing dependence on alcohol and drugs. "Drugs are a way of pulling back while still being in front of people," he said. "Your world contracts to the size of your nostril." It was expensive too. As he said at the time, "Cocaine is God's way of telling you you're making too much móney."

In March of 1982, when his friend and fellow comedian John Belushi died of a cocaine and heroin overdose, Williams was distraught. He regarded Belushi as a kindred spirit who had shared his love of the comedy of Jonathan Winters. That fall, Williams left Los Angeles and settled down on a ranch in northern California. In 1983 Zachary was born to him and Valerie Velardi, a dancer he married in 1978. (They have since separated.)

In his Metropolitan Opera concert, Robin told how he had said good-by to drugs and alcohol to set a good example for his son:

"Now that you have a child, you have to clean up your act. You can't come home drunk and go, 'Hey, here's a little switch—Daddy's gonna throw up on *you.'*" And "you don't need drugs when you have a kid—you're awake, you're paranoid, you smell bad—it's the same thing!"

When not performing, Robin lives quietly on his Napa Valley ranch, where he reads, runs and plays with Zachary, who lives with him part-time. "When I was in Thailand making *Good Morning, Vietnam*, I'd stay up all night to make a call at five in the morning in Bangkok, to reach Zachary at three in the afternoon, or I'd figure out how I could get him right when he woke up by calculating the 15-hour time difference, plus daylight-saving time, plus travel time to the telephone, to say, 'Hey, Zach! Daddy loves you!' And he says: 'I can't talk now, I'm eating breakfast and *He-Man* is on. Bye!'"

On the Road. When I spent four days with Robin in New York last summer, he seemed to have a 56-hour energy charge. On a typical day, he jogged, then shopped for books (ranging from the latest Saul Bellow novel to two new Russian novels to a book on the brain to the latest Heavy Metal comic book). In the evening he caught an Off-Broadway play and gave a dinner for some friends. At midnight he dropped in unannounced at The Improvisation Club to do an hour of spontaneous comedy, then took a crowd of people to an all-night restaurant where he talked to them in a bewildering variety of styles and accents.

On another day, in an elegant Manhattan restaurant, he conversed in his normal speaking voice, which is soft and almost English-sounding in its clipped precision. But when he was asked about the jungle scene in his latest film, he suddenly reproduced insect noises in very loud, compact-disc fidelity. Heads turned. Obviously people had never heard authentic jungle sounds at the restaurant before.

What I found most remarkable about the man was his sweetness. He shows an interest in everybody and everything around him. Then, as his relentless curiosity takes over, he makes connections between what he sees and hears, and things in his head that don't seem related at all — until he shows us the link we have missed.

Besides unexpected connections, just what is his weird humor all about? "I use comedy to confront people's fears," Williams says. "I can say, 'I'm as scared as you are, but I have an interesting view and I think we can get through this together.'"

And no doubt we can.

Solution

Analysis: The opening anecdote of the child's face gets the reader into the general statement, which seems to be that Williams produces unexpected but exactly right lines and faces. The Buckley/Mace/Rogers skits seem to be three points of justification then, after the word "Armageddon," we start amplification, Now-stuff that has happened in this phase of his life — movies, records, and so forth. The subhead "Coming-Out Party" (1) seems to begin flashback. But where was wart? Flashback runs up to how he got part as Mork that brought him national recognition (2). The drugs and booze are a clear wart, and this leads neatly into more now-stuff about his relations with son. Then we have a interlude of day spent with author of article, and a final quote about Williams's appeal. *Recommendations:* Two or three dozen students in my senior/graduate level editing classes have studied this article closely, and a general consensus emerged on a number of points. First, they felt the lead was serviceable but lackluster. If the purpose is to show Williams as a genius of improvisation then two far more dramatic incidents commended themselves: the clicking jungle sounds in a restaurant (3) or, better still, the dumping of the scripts in *Good Morning Vietnam* (4) and using his crazy ad-libs instead; perhaps material for such a lead can be taken from the Mr. Leo skit in the box? A number of my students thought the general statement could be broadened beyond master of the *mot juste* to the creator of a whole new kind of manic humor. This, in turn, would broaden the three points of justification from three rather similar skits to diverse achievements on stage, films, and records. There are also some possible sparks in the fact that, unlike many stand-up comedians, Williams seems extraordinarily well educated and well read. Also, unlike many famous people on the fast track, he seems to be a very nice man. On the whole, the students felt the flashback section, with Williams's struggle to unveil his talent, both dramatic and effective. The drug wart was well-handled, and funny. But what of the second wart? A strong possibility could be the break-up of his marriage after so short a time. Also, there's the near-frenzied (too frenzied?) visit to New York (5). No profile *has* to have two, or more, warts; but the article as it stands leaves some questions that need to be answered. Finally, it lacks all mention of whither. My students, and readers generally, must have wondered what this extraordinary man was going to do next. Star in a musical? Write a book on existentialism? Sail round the world?

7

STORY ORGANIZATION 2
Do-It-Yourself, Trends,
and Disasters

IF ROBERT RUARK had downed a few more vodka martinis that day in the International Club, then undoubtedly Bill Roberts's den would now be decorated with diagrams detailing the organization structure of all major types of magazine article. As it is, we are left with a quotation from a character in Ruark's autobiographical novel *The Honeybadger* who observes that "every good magazine piece has just as much architectural form as a building or any other precise structure."

What, then, are the architectural forms of such major story types as the service or how-to, the human interest, and the information, or trend?

SERVICE, OR HOW-TO

The kind of story least likely to tax the waning sobriety of Ruark and Roberts would surely have been the service piece. Here the writer simply outlines a problem of concern to the reader and then enumerates ways in which it can be resolved. Such a form is staple fare for most magazines with specialized readerships. Examples are:

ALTERNATIVE LIGHT STYLES
Enlightenment in the world of gas and kerosene lamps.
Harrowsmith, October 1980

The Canadian back-to-the-land magazine *Harrowsmith* is helping its readers resolve their home lighting problems, in the same way that *Cruising*

World magazine is helping its adventurous readers pilot a large sailboat through perilous northern waters with

CRUISING THE GULF OF ALASKA
Summer amidst the bergy bits concludes with a shaky landfall.
Cruising World, May 1980

Here are a couple of other examples of how-to-articles:

GETTING ALONG IN
A NONSEXIST FAMILY
Ms., October 1980

THE ARTFUL PICKUP.
A SIMPLE TECHNIQUE TO ATTRACT THE
RIGHT MAN (HE'LL BE DEFENSELESS!)
Cosmopolitan, December 1980

Since the problems mentioned above are generally familiar to the specialized readerships, it does not call for a great deal of editorial salesmanship to get readers into the piece. If you don't want to attract the "right man" then you are not going to fool around with the Artful Pickup. But if you do, you're going to be in there reading hard and all the writer needs to do is make a rotelike exposition of solutions. Six new ways to light your home. Sixteen new ways to pick up a man.

Just as an anecdote is a specially effective way to open a personality profile, a particularly effective way to open a service piece is the recap lead (see chap. 5), as seen below for a how-to article entitled *Condomania: Hot Buys in 7 Cities:*

> Ten years ago, few of us ever imagined that our someday dream house might well be located in a multimillion dollar high-rise commune. Words like condo and co-op were new to our vocabulary then, and communal living had an entirely different connotation. Now, international real estate consultant Robert C. Lesser of Los Angeles predicts that condominiums "tolerated in the Sixties and accepted in the Seventies, will replace the traditional single family house as the preferred home of the Eighties." He's hardly alone in his assessment of things to come.
>
> GENERAL STATEMENT
>
> Government and industry experts alike agree about two startling things: One, in 20 years half the U.S. population could be living in owned multi-family dwellings; two, if you're thinking of buying there's no time like the present—unless it was yesterday.

Apartment Life, November 1980

The lead recaps the old ways before telling us condos are in, and here are some smart ways to get one without losing your shirt.

HUMAN INTEREST

The organization of this kind of story is more complicated, but it has a close affinity to the personality profile. By its nature the human interest story (big things about little people) generally concerns itself with some predicament or disaster that is not caused directly by the participants. A fire traps hundreds in a swank Las Vegas hotel. More than one hundred men die when an oil rig tips over in the North Sea. A nuclear power plant melts down, causing the evacuation of thousands. Or a man and his three daughters survive a blizzard after their plane crashes high in the Rockies. The cause does not come from within; it is Fate dicing with the lives of innocent victims.

This kind of story is a natural for outdoors or adventure publications. But a piece on how a whole mountain blew up, or how a kidnap victim was forced to become a human bomb, can appeal to a more general audience. So much so that *Reader's Digest* has a continuing series — entitled "Drama in Real Life" — devoted to chronicling the heroism and the fortitude of these sagas. A Ruarkian analysis of *Digest*'s "Dramas" shows them to have a tightly structured format that looks something like the diagram shown in figure 8. We shall illustrate this pattern by taking examples from a real-life drama entitled "Ordeal at Hell's Hole," appearing in the November 1980 issue of the *Digest*. The story relates the experiences of an amateur pilot named Barry Krieger, aged forty-one, whose Piper Apache crashed 12,000 feet up in the Rockies two days before Christmas, 1979. With Krieger were his aged mother-in-law and his three daughters, aged sixteen, fifteen, and ten. When the plane hit the mountain the mother-in-law died instantly, and Krieger's legs were paralyzed. The plane's emergency location transmitter went on immediately, but a blizzard prevented rescuers from reaching the plane until the next day. The family kept alive in the intense cold by rubbing one another's limbs and reading the Bible out loud. At one point Krieger became delirious and ordered his daughters to set fire to the plane. They disobeyed him. On another occasion, the fifteen-year-old girl crawled to a nearby ridge through 80-m.p.h. winds and 40-degree-below-zero temperatures to seek help, all with two crushed vertebrae in her back. The next day the weather cleared and the family were rescued by helicopter. Mr. Krieger underwent surgery for a broken back and both his frostbitten legs had to be amputated below the knee. Despite all manner of troubles, however, the human interest story must have an upbeat ending. Examine, now, how these elements are assembled on the Facts side of the diagram.

FORM

FACTS

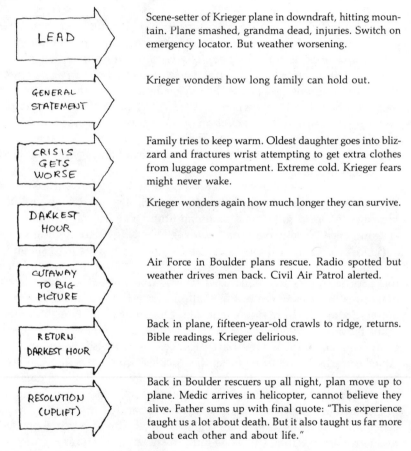

LEAD

Scene-setter of Krieger plane in downdraft, hitting mountain. Plane smashed, grandma dead, injuries. Switch on emergency locator. But weather worsening.

GENERAL STATEMENT

Krieger wonders how long family can hold out.

CRISIS GETS WORSE

Family tries to keep warm. Oldest daughter goes into blizzard and fractures wrist attempting to get extra clothes from luggage compartment. Extreme cold. Krieger fears might never wake.

DARKEST HOUR

Krieger wonders again how much longer they can survive.

CUTAWAY TO BIG PICTURE

Air Force in Boulder plans rescue. Radio spotted but weather drives men back. Civil Air Patrol alerted.

RETURN DARKEST HOUR

Back in plane, fifteen-year-old crawls to ridge, returns. Bible readings. Krieger delirious.

RESOLUTION (UPLIFT)

Back in Boulder rescuers up all night, plan move up to plane. Medic arrives in helicopter, cannot believe they alive. Father sums up with final quote: "This experience taught us a lot about death. But it also taught us far more about each other and about life."

Fig. 8. Breakdown of human interest story.

Human interest stories do not, as a rule, open with a personal anecdote. It is more likely that a description of the incident or "trigger" event that sets the story in motion will be used. Here is the lead for the *Digest's* real-life drama "Death in the North Sea."

On the *Alexander L. Kielland*, a huge, floating dormitory platform among the drilling rigs in the North Sea's Greater Ekofisk oil field, the day shift had just come off duty. Dozens of men went straight to the dining hall for the evening meal. Sixty or more flocked into the rig's cinema. Outside a gale was tossing twenty-five-foot waves against the platform's legs. No cause for concern. The *Kielland* was considered a marvel of modern engineering, designed to withstand any weather, with watertight compartments in the legs and pontoons.

Suddenly a shudder came from deep below. The men at the movie cheered; an anchor chain might have broken, meaning a day off for many while repairs were made. The cheering choked in their throats as another shudder was followed by a loud bang and the room tilted to a perilous angle of 30 degrees, then 40. The movie screen lurched upward to become the ceiling, chairs plunged down into the rear exits. A ping-pong table from the adjoining recreation room and heavy rig equipment crashed through the thin wall into the movie hall to crush many of the screaming men scrambling to reach the doors.

GENERAL {Thus at 6:29 P.M. last March 27, began the worst disaster in the his-
STATEMENT {tory of offshore oil exploration.

Reader's Digest, October 1980

The account goes on to document the chaos on the platform, how some men got out, while 123 were crushed or drowned. Some lifeboats were destroyed, and others could not be launched. Some men sought to save their comrades while others panicked. The writer followed the particular experiences of Tom Greenwood through the disaster. Greenwood helped launch a lifeboat, but it capsized and the men were left in the freezing water holding onto bits of wreckage. At this point, the writer cuts away to the rescue attempts by the air forces of both Britain and Norway. We follow the helicopters back to the wreckage and the "darkest hour." After some technical explanation, the *Digest* ends on an upbeat tone:

> The loss of 123 men on the *Alexander L. Keilland,* tragic as it was, may help to save the lives of other men braving the North Sea.

The human interest story has one major structural difference from the personality profile. In the profile, the high points of the article are logically connected with the subject's history. But in a human interest story (unless, of course, you adopt the mystical view expounded by Thornton Wilder in his wonderful *Bridge of San Luis Rey*), there is little or no logical connection between the great disaster and the personal histories of its victims. Thus, instead of a flashback section, we have an account of the "big picture." It is in this section that the writer steps back from the darkest hour to examine matters about which the victims know little or nothing. As we have seen from the example of the plane crash and the oil-rig disaster, these might include technical explanations of the storm/crash/meltdown, the top-level decisions to deal with it, rescue attempts, the concern of relatives, and so forth. Having explained the "big picture," the writer then takes his readers back into the "darkest hour" and the center of the personal drama.

One of the chief problems presented by disaster stories is their breadth. A detailed portrayal of the demise of each of 123 oil-rig victims, or even a detailed account of the experiences of each of the sixty-odd survivors, can leave the readers both numb and confused. Thus the first task of the writer or editor is to bring the mass of material into an understandable focus. This is most effectively done by concentrating on the experience of a single *typical* family or victim. It was in this fashion that the *Digest* selected Tom Greenwood from among the survivors of the oil-rig disaster. He showed courage, but not so much courage that he becomes a hero — for that would be a different kind of story: How Tom Greenwood Saved Sixty Oil-riggers Singlehanded. For this reason, digging out the family or individual whose experiences best typify those of all the victims becomes an editorial task of primary importance. The selection is critical, for it dominates the tone of the article; at the same time it must be founded upon a great deal of preliminary research, for only after that has been done can the writer have a sense of what is typical.

TRENDS

The last major type of story is the informative-news story. Most of the material in this kind of story is presented in the daily newspaper and set in the format of the inverted pyramid. But there is one major type of story in this category that is used by both newspapers and magazines: the trend story. The variety of topics is without limit. The "trend" may be a surge in high school vandalism, a series of developments in dental surgery, or a new mode in abstract art. The discovery and documentation of such trends represent one of the most exciting — and most exacting — forms of magazine journalism.

The trend story is exciting because, unlike most magazine stories, it is not foreshadowed in the pages of the newspapers. It can offer the reader wholly new insights on society and the way we live and work. At the same time the trend story is exacting because it presents special problems in both research and organization.

The personality profile is, in a sense, one-dimensional. It calls for solid research into a single topic. This is represented visually in figure 9,*a*. In contrast, a trend story often requires the documentation of a series of 5 and 10 percent changes across a broad spectrum of subjects, as shown in figure 9,*b*. Let's say you are working on a major trend story like the

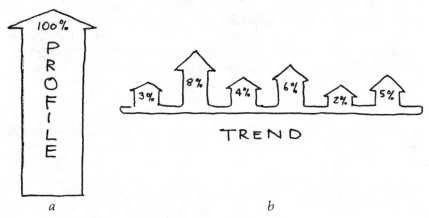

a   *b*

Fig. 9. Comparing trends and personality profiles.

one that appeared in the November 23, 1980, issue of the *New York Times Magazine:* "The New Extended Family: Divorce Reshapes the American Household." For this story, or one of similar complexity, you have interviewed families in a dozen cities and spoken with sociologists, psychologists, and marriage counselors across the country. Your research findings and quotes fill half a dozen notebooks and as many tapes. Finally, the time has come to put it all together and write an article. Your editor has given you a deadline. You take the phone off the hook, slide a piece of paper into the typewriter—and go blank.

The material seems overwhelming in both quantity and variety. After 5 minutes of staring at the wall, you go to the kitchen to make coffee, only to see a memo written to yourself: "Joan needs first draft July 12." It is now July 8. Panic sets in. How, you wonder, can I possibly organize this mountain of material into a coherent article? Maybe I'd be better off driving a hack, or teaching.

Much of this apprehension can be dissipated if you realize that, like the personality profile and the human interest story, there is also a clear logical structure for a trend piece. The *Wall Street Journal* has long been renowned for its page-one trend stories. Henry Fairlie, the British critic, has pronounced them among the best-written pieces of journalism in America. With this accolade in mind, a graduate student and I resolved to analyze these stories to see if a common organizational form lay beneath the *WSJ*'s immense variety of trend topics. We read more than 1,000 leader columns in all. But we had not looked at more than 100 before we discerned, amid great excitement, a clear pattern of organization. When I wrote up our findings for the *Columbia Journalism Review* (Fall 1968) I called this pattern the DEE-System of organization.

The publication of our study, however, did not have quite the astounding effect I expected. I received a note from the chief editorial writer at the *Journal*, who said that the formulation of the DEE-System had not helped his writers at all; indeed, it had given many of them a savage case of "writer's block." The analysis was not wrong, said the editor. It was, in truth, devastatingly accurate. Up until that time his very gifted writers had assembled their material by hunch, a process of intuitive judgments based on years of experience. This quote here, that statistic there. Why? Because it "felt right." When I dug out the principles implicit in this process, and made them explicit, the new voice from without jangled up the old voice from within. Result: half a dozen lobotomized wordsmiths.

It is therefore with some trepidation that I offer you the DEE-System. It may work effectively for you; unlike the old pros at the *WSJ*, you do not yet have a voice of extensive experience speaking to you from within. If you did have that voice then you would not be looking in mortal panic at the memo pinned to your kitchen wall telling you "Joan needs first draft July 12."

The first requirement of the DEE-System is that the writer (or editor) must state the main thrust of the trend with the utmost clarity. Admittedly, this is often hard to do. You are writing a story about the new extended family. You note that there are 3.5 million American households, or about one in every seven, which have at least one parent and one child from a previous marriage. Also, that more than one in three marriages in the 1980s will end in divorce, and by 1990 only about half of all children under eighteen will be living with both their natural parents. Your original idea for a main thrust had been: *Surge in Extended Families.* But now the statistic mentioned above dangles another possibility in front of you: *Surge in Divorces.*

These two stories are closely connected, and can probably be written from the same body of facts. Some writers and editors might try to fudge them together but, and they are likely to find out the hard way, this will plunge the article into organizational chaos. There is surely a place for all these facts in a well-constructed story, but there can be no coherent organization until it is decided what the main thrust is to be. A trend story that attempts to juggle two main thrusts runs about as smoothly as a wheel with two axles, or a country with two kings.

When the main thrust has been determined, the material of the article can then be keyed into the following organizational categories: *description* of main thrust, *explanation* of main thrust, and *evaluation* of main thrust (see fig. 10). These three categories — description, explanation, and evaluation — account for the name of the DEE-System.

The most effective lead for a trend story is generally a roundup, or bullet, lead, since it enables the writer to delineate the spread of events making up the trend. But an anecdotal lead often works well, too. The *Times Magazine* piece on extended families opened with color shots of three such families (one in California, one in Alabama, and one with eighteen people in a swimming pool in Iowa), but its text led off with a detailed account of the California family and how it fitted together. Having shown the diversity of the trend phenomenon, the writer moved into the general statement that propounds the main thrust of the trend:

> Created by divorce and remarriage, and common to millions of Americans in every section of the country and on every rung of the social and economic ladder, the new American extended family has attracted the attention of social scientists nationwide. In the first flurry . . .
>
> *New York Times Magazine*, November 23, 1980

Description

The next category of data must now *describe* the surge in extended families by presenting statistics from different agencies and surveys made in different parts of the country. In what age groups and occupations is it highest? How is it increasing over previous years and decades? A good way to conclude the descriptive section and to give life to the mass of statistics is to use a colorful, and even opinionated, quote by an acknowledged authority in the field.

Explanation

In this section you present all the material that *explains* the surge. Motives and sociological changes often play a big part here, and you may wish to cast back into the past to discover the roots of the present trend. Quotes from sociologists and historians and psychological experts are in

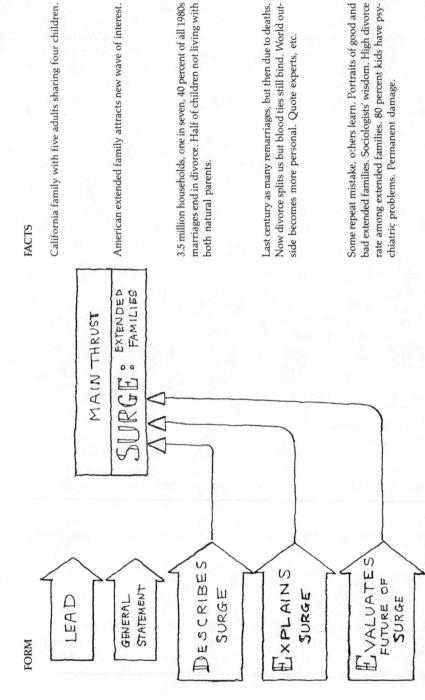

FACTS

California family with five adults sharing four children.

American extended family attracts new wave of interest.

3.5 million households, one in seven, 40 percent of all 1980s marriages end in divorce. Half of children not living with both natural parents.

Last century as many remarriages, but then due to deaths. Now divorce splits us but blood ties still bind. World outside becomes more personal. Quote experts, etc.

Some repeat mistake, others learn. Portraits of good and bad extended families. Sociologists' wisdom. High divorce rate among extended families. 80 percent kids have psychiatric problems. Permanent damage.

FORM

LEAD

GENERAL STATEMENT

MAIN THRUST

SURGE: EXTENDED FAMILIES

DESCRIBES SURGE

EXPLAINS SURGE

EVALUATES FUTURE OF SURGE

Fig. 10. Structure of a trend story.

order. The economic and religious climate may also have played a role in the development of the trend you are documenting.

Evaluation

Here you evaluate the future of the trend. The tone is avowedly speculative. Will the proportion of extended marriages increase or decrease? How will the trend look by the year 2000? What factors are likely to affect the change? Are new values likely to inhibit or accelerate the trend? Will it be affected by legislation? A change in the tax laws? Once again, quotations from authorities are in order. And if they disagree with one another, their views should be clearly contrasted. A major segment of the *Times'* article on extended families was devoted to examining and evaluating the impact of new relationships on the three sample families. What did their experiences, good and bad, show the readers about the future shape of society?

The DEE-System, when rigorously applied, can cut the time an editor devotes to organizing material by 70 percent. When a writer is sifting through half a dozen books of notes, the organizational process can be speeded by the use of three different-colored pens — red for description, blue for explanation, and so on. Then, when it comes to writing description, all the red-ticked material can be keyed on to a single sheet of paper and both writer and editor can proceed in a systematic fashion. Material, however, need not remain locked in a particular organizational category. In the *Times* story, for instance, the data on the rising proportion of children not living with both their natural parents could be used in the explanation (children are seemingly willing to get along with stepparents) or in the evaluation (Will the figure increase in the future? Will these extended-family children suffer emotional damage? Will they lead society back to a rigid Victorian family ethic?). The editor should be prepared to use the material in the segment where it helps the story most.

Problems

One final comment about the DEE-System. It is such an efficient organizer of material that some of its admirers have been tempted to take shortcuts in their research. They decide what the trend is, then do the minimal research to plausibly fill each of the three organizational categories, and then write up a storm. The only problem is that if they had troubled to do more extensive research they might have found that their original idea of a trend was not valid. The contrary, even, may be true.

Writers and editors new to the DEE-System often make the mistake of failing to apply the organizational categories to the main thrust. Instead, they apply them to the subject matter itself. That is to say, they attempt to describe or explain extended marriages, instead of applying them to the *surge* in extended marriages. This may seem like a subtle point, but it can make all the difference between chaos and a semblance of order.

There is as clear a logic to the DEE-System as there is to any of the organizational forms — try explaining a trend before you have described it. But a closer look at the diagrams shows a strong resemblance to the personality profile. Both are divided into three main blocks. And, in both cases, the first block is set in the present, the second in the past, and the third in the future. Both, if you will, move from the concrete to the abstract. Nothing is more concrete than the present. The past is more abstract, but it has the concreteness of being a previous present. And the future is most abstract of all because it has yet to happen.

ASSIGNMENT 1

Read through the following article from the January 1981 *Good Housekeeping* and see if you can analyze it into its component parts. Note the paragraphs that set the drama in motion, the "darkest hour," the "cutaway," and the return to the darkest hour, together with the upbeat end. Could the material have been better organized? If so, how would you have done it?

THE TOWN THAT SAVED A LITTLE BOY

by Judy Passmore McNeal

Martin Mallo is alive because the people of Ambler, Pa., would not let him die.

When I first met Martin Mallo, he was two years old, full of energy and curiosity. His big brown eyes took in everything around him. He was an adorable picture of health. But Martin was not what he seemed. The little boy from La Paz, Bolivia, had cancer, and there was a good chance he'd lose his sight and perhaps his life to the disease.

Today, however, two years later, Martin is alive and growing fast—thanks to an amazing outpouring of love and concern from the people of my hometown, Ambler, Pa. My friends and neighbors took Martin to their hearts and got him the very best medical treatment money can buy.

It all started in 1977 in Martin's hometown in Bolivia when the little boy was just 16 months old. His mother, Magaly, noticed that one of her son's eyes would "drift." She took him to an eye doctor, who diagnosed the problem as *retinoblastoma*, a rare form of cancer that causes malignant tumors to form on the retina of the eye. Because the disease is difficult to treat, the doctor told Magaly to take her son to see Dr. Robert Ellsworth at the eye-tumor clinic of Columbia Presbyterian Hospital in New York City.

For Magaly Mallo, an unemployed social worker, a trip to New York seemed impossible. Air fare alone would cost more than $1,200. Because she had no choice, she gathered all her savings and bought two round-trip tickets to the United States.

In the autumn of 1977 Magaly and Martin arrived in New York City. Not knowing a soul, she somehow managed to find Dr. Ellsworth and Columbia Presbyterian Hospital. How she managed is a mystery, but mothers of sick children have their own special brand of bravery.

Magaly got a room at Reese House (a residence for families of patients) two blocks from the hospital and, for the next two months, she and Martin lived a hand-to-mouth existence. For Magaly it was a lonely, frightening time. Christmas and New Year's came and went without much celebration. No one else at Reese House spoke her language, and Magaly knew no English. With no real friends, she spent most days alone, while Martin underwent radiation treatment in both eyes, followed by cryotherapy (a freezing technique). Dr. Ellsworth hoped that by diminishing the size of the tumors, he would be able to save some of the child's vision.

Soon the $800 Magaly had had when she arrived was almost gone. She wrote a discouraged letter to her father in Bolivia, who, in turn, wrote a letter to some distant cousins in the town where I live, Ambler, Pa.

In February 1978 Ambler resident Lidia Salazar received the letter from Magaly's father. She and her husband, Nestor, drove to New York and took Magaly and Martin home to Ambler.

Magaly used the last of her money to buy dried fruit as a gift for her hosts.

Magaly told Lidia and Nestor that Martin needed to undergo treatment every three months for the next two years. If his eyes did not respond to this treatment they would have to be removed because the disease is often fatal if it spreads beyond the eyes.

Though Dr. Ellsworth had agreed to work without a fee, hospital costs at that time were approximately $300 a day. Added to this was the cost of the room at Reese House and food. Deeply distressed, Magaly told the Salazars that she had no money—and no idea where to get any.

Word about Martin spread through Ambler. A small committee was formed headed by Sophia Darian, a neighbor of the Salazars. Sophia asked me and four other friends to join.

We held our first meeting in March, and while we were asking Magaly questions about Bolivia (using Lidia as an interpreter) a little of the young mother's bravery dissolved, and she began to weep. Then Lidia

"Our town put the story of the Good Samaritan to everyday use. Maybe yours can too"

started to cry too. When she finally steadied her voice, she blurted out. "Magaly is afraid Martin is going to die."

It was probably the first time Magaly had allowed herself to say those words. By then we were all crying. Martin who had been playing quietly, climbed onto his mother's lap and tried to kiss away her tears.

The first to regain composure was Jo-

Ann Sigmund. She knelt by Magaly's chair and said to Lidia "Tell Magaly we will help in any way we can. We are her friends."

When Magaly heard this she nodded and said, "Maybe God has not forgotten us after all."

Each of us had at some time been a fund raiser. We'd all put posters in local store windows or collected door prizes for charity affairs. But none had ever raised money so that a small child could live. Now we felt inspired. We set our goal at $15,000 and never doubted for a minute that we could make it.

JoAnn's husband, Pete, suggested that Ambler "adopt" Martin. Ted Thompson, our lawyer, arranged for a TV news crew to film the borough council when it approved the adoption proposition. The next morning the story ran in newspapers around the state. Suddenly the Martin Paul Mallo Fund was snowballing.

Schoolchildren made and sold popcorn, organized cake sales, and painted posters to be placed in store windows. A check for $100 came in the same mail with 73 cents. One child sent the contents of his piggy bank, along with a religious medal. In two weeks we had raised $2,000.

Then a local car dealer offered to sponsor a "Happy Birthday, Martin" sale. He pledged $25 to the fund for every car and truck he sold or delivered that weekend.

Another merchant wrote to all of Ambler's store owners, saying that during one week in June he planned to donate two percent of his profits on all sales. He concluded his letter with these words: "Hurry, a little boy is waiting." Almost 70 merchants pitched in and contributed $2,500.

Now we had $7,000 for Martin, almost half our original goal.

Meanwhile, Martin and his mother had gone back to Bolivia to work out their visas. They were expected back in Ambler in July. For their return, Ted Thompson began organizing a huge adoption celebration. Sixty posters with Martin's picture were distributed to shopkeepers. Volunteers lettered a huge

welcoming banner and hung it across Butler Street. Handwritten thank-you notes (more than 450 in all) went out to those who had sent donations. A ceremony was planned to take place in the chapel of St. Mary's Home, and the 45-piece Wissahicken High School band practiced the Bolivian national anthem.

We even obtained visas for Magaly and Martin, permitting them to stay in the United States for an extended period. The hard-to-get visas came about because Pete Sigmund is related by marraige to Congresswoman Lindy Boggs of Louisiana. Through her efforts and the kind understanding of the U.S. Ambassador to Bolivia, one-year visas were issued to the Mallos.

So many logistical problems had to be settled that we sometimes lost track of the little boy involved. And though we didn't say it, we knew there were still no guarantees that Martin could be saved.

Of the 15 children Dr. Ellsworth had under treatment in New York at that time, only two had not had to have at least one eye removed. Martin was one of them. We had never let ourselves consider anything less than a perfect Martin, yet as the time for his return neared, I think we all prayed even harder than usual.

On July 9, 1978, the long-awaited adoption celebration went off beautifully. In the chapel at St. Mary's, little Martin was made an honorary son of Ambler by Mayor George Saurman, who also presented him with a key to the city — the first one ever presented.

Magaly had composed her own speech of thanks and read it to the 200 people present. It was a touching moment. Outside, in the hot July sun, the bank struck up the theme song from the movie *Rocky*.

The next day Magaly took Martin to see Dr. Ellsworth in New York. We waited with bated breath for the outcome. We need not have worried. When the doctor examined Martin he found that the tumors had not grown — he would not need to see the child again until October.

When that news appeared in the town paper one could practically *hear* the sigh of relief. The look on people's faces seemed to say, "Thank goodness, maybe our boy is going to be okay."

In October Martin's tumors were still under control, so we sent Martin and Magaly back to Bolivia for the holidays.

Early in 1979 Magaly and Martin returned to Ambler so the boy could continue his cryotherapy and radiation treatments. All went well until November, when Martin's left eye stopped responding to treatment. The invading cancer cells were multiplying rapidly. The doctors had no choice—they had to remove the left eye. The operation was a success, and Martin has since been fitted with a prosthesis.

Martin and his mother now live in Norristown, Pa., where Martin, four, attends nursery school.

Some children have been completely cured of retinoblastoma; others have needed treatment for as long as nine years. We all are praying that Martin will be one of the lucky ones.

Ambler, our sleepy, blue-collar town of 8,000 persons, has put the story of the Good Samaritan to everyday use. Any town could do it. Have you looked around yours?

A child may be waiting.

Solution

This is not a mechanical disaster, but the lead paragraph confronts readers with a paradox—a seemingly healthy child who in fact has cancer that may take his sight and his life. But—and now we have the general statement of the article's theme—he was saved from this fate by Ambler, Pa. townspeople who took Martin to their hearts and got medical treatment (1). We then cut away to the first troubles building to Magaly's difficulties in New York (2). Darkest hour no. 1 comes when her $800 is gone and she writes a hopeless letter home (3). Then we cut away to "big picture." Lidia Salazar gets a letter and a committee is formed; Magaly and Martin are then brought to Ambler (4) and the drive for $15,000 proceeds (5). But there is a neat transition—"So many logistical problems had to be settled that we sometimes lost track of the little boy involved"—takes us back to the "darkest hour" (6). The town adopts Martin but then he must have one eye removed. This sounds a gloomy note, but somehow the writer grabs for an upbeat ending in the good works of the people of Ambler.

ASSIGNMENT 2

Read the following trend story from *Newsweek* (April 16, 1979) and identify the main thrust (general statement) and descriptive, explanatory, and evaluative sections, noting where arrangements differ from the DEE form. Would the story be improved if the "errant" material were placed in its logically correct place?

URBAN ARCHEOLOGY

Clearing a site for Atlanta's new subway system several years ago, construction workers made an unexpected find. Buried in an old garbage dump were the remains of a community called Edgewood which had existed from 1897 to 1910. The tiny town had been forgotten by local historians, but its tale was preserved in its trash. As archeologists sifted through the heap, they were able to determine when residents switched from kerosene to electricity, when they dropped patent medicines in favor of prescription drugs and what cuts of meat they favored: curiously enough, animal heads and feet. Judging from the number of whisky jugs, some Edgewoodians also honored local prohibition laws mainly in the breach — and by the gallon. "People's garbage never lies," explains Georgia State Prof. Roy Dickens, head of

1 the Atlanta dig. "It tells the truth if you know how to read it."

Although many archeologists wouldn't trade a dig in ancient Sumer for all the trash

2 heaps in Georgia, a new breed of explorers is dredging up history right in the heart of the modern city. Some of the finds are imposing: urban archeologists have salvaged

3 a Revolutionary War tavern from a Brooklyn sewer and a vast deposit of Indian crockery in Harvard Square. More often, city salvage tends toward such run-of-the-mill relics as food remains, abandoned privy pits or a cache of "The Great Dr. Kilmer's Swamp Root." But even these finds, say archeologists, provide clues to a city's past and progress. "Instead of looking for the place where

Ben Franklin lived, we're studying the total city as a site," explains Pamela Cressey, head of the Archaeology Research Center of Alexandria, Va. "It's archeology *of* the city, not just in it."

"Under Their Feet": City digs are in   4 part a search for roots and a symptom of the current urban-preservation fever. "People are wondering what their ancestors were like," explains Mark Barnes, an archeologist with the U.S. Department of the Interior. "And it's all there under their feet." Alexandria's municipal archeological research center was created when residents began to fear that the city's past was being destroyed by redevelopment. In the past year and a half, 250 volunteers have helped archeologists re-   6 trieve more than 800,000 artifacts dating from 1749, when the city was settled. The new field has also been aided by a series of Federal laws requiring that Federally funded projects — like the construction of Atlanta's rail system — be preceded by an archeological survey. If excavations are needed to recover archeological resources, the government will help pay the bill.

By studying written records and identifying castoffs, archeologists can reconstruct trade and migration patterns and trace changes in land use and social status. Last summer, excavators in Portsmouth, N.H., showed how a seventeenth-century Indian campsite evolved into an eighteenth-century maritime commercial district and eventually into a twentieth-century slum until its renovation twenty years ago. Researchers working in Newburyport, Mass., discovered needles, pulleys and a stencil belonging to a family of sailmakers called Davis. Artifacts recovered from the site showed that when rail service was introduced in 1872, the Davises converted their sail business to the production of awnings. Ink bottles and slate pencils gathered from another dig in Newburyport showed that some of the "illiterate" Irish and Canadian immigrants recorded by census takers could actually read and write.

The city digs are reviving much of the lost history of the working-class poor. An old Irish section was uncovered in Detroit several years ago when archeologists found a clay-pipe factory. In Birmingham, Mich., workers unearthed a tile-making factory from the 1850s. "All tile was made by hand then," says anthropologist Arnold Pilling of Wayne State University. "But in Birmingham, a man had made a machine to produce tile." In the industrial city of Paterson, N.J., researchers are reconstructing the life-styles of the factory workers. "It's not the Mayflower or the heroes of the revolution," concedes archeologist Ed Rutsch. "But we are what we are because of Paterson."

Important Clues: Archeologists claim 5
a clearer picture of the urban past can help solve current city problems. "Once we begin to see how older urban societies reacted to different conditions — to scarce resources, to unexpected climatic changes — we can understand more about our current cultural experiences," says Mike Roberts of the Institute for Conservation Archaeology at Harvard's Peabody Museum. And even in its primitive stages, urban archeology has provided important clues to unraveling the past. Directed by Robert Schuyler, of New York's City College, archeologists have been excavating the site of Weeksville, a nineteenth-century black settlement located in Brooklyn. Today, local schools use Weeksville artifacts to teach black history and the community is trying to restore three Weeksville houses to a neighborhood museum. "A lot of people think we're just a bunch of black people trying to do something exotic," says Joan Maynard, director of the Society for the Preservation of Weeksville. "But we have to use all available sources to piece together our history." As it turns out, what was omitted in history texts was often simply thrown out with the trash.

Solution

We have a scene-setter lead opening on Edgewood, nailed down at the end of the first paragraph by a bright quote from Professor Dickens (1). Then the main thrust of the trend is announced in the first sentence of the second paragraph with "a new breed of explorers is dredging up history" (2) and description of that surge follows with the Brooklyn sewer, Harvard Yard, and Dr. Kilmer (3). Note the diversity of these examples, giving the story geographical spread. Explanation starts with "City digs are in part a search for" (4). Though the dope on Portsmouth, N.H. could serve in the descriptive section it is in this section because it helps explain the motives of the searchers. Evaluation begins with "Important Clues" (5). Clearly, there is some descriptive material in the explanatory section. The fact that 250 volunteers have sifted 800,000 artifacts (6) would give numerical substance to the description of the trend. The sentence does not disrupt explanation, but it would clearly serve the writer better in description.

8

EDITING 1

Heads, Decks, and the
Changing of the Palace Guard

WHEN IS A GUARDSMAN NOT A GRENADIER but a Coldstream? On the answer to that esoteric question hung the issue of whether I should be fired from the staff of the *National Geographic* or be permitted to continue as a very junior writer in the Legends Department of the magazine. The *Geographic* quaintly calls its picture captions "legends" and it was my job to write, and double-check, all the material that went into the captions accompanying a particular article. Much artistry goes into the composition of legends. Not many of *National Geographic*'s subscribers read the entire text of a piece; instead, they coast through the article by skipping from legend to legend, and these must thus carry the story.

I had been assigned to write the captions for an article from the London bureau on the opening by Queen Elizabeth of a new session of Parliament. The colorful ceremony had been taking place for nearly a thousand years, but this was the first occasion on which cameras were to be permitted to photograph the speech from the throne. The pictures were loaded with the fabulous crimsons and gold lace of heraldic attire. Crowned royalty rode through the crowds in Cinderella coaches. Periwigged peers and their ladies, decked out in ermine, jammed into the House of Lords to hear the Queen speak. It was a great piece, but as we prepared it for publication back in the magazine's Washington office, we quickly ran into trouble.

After going through scores of magnificent slides, the picture editor's final choice included a shot of Coldstream guards, with their big bearskin hats protecting the line of procession, and a handsome shot of several aristocratic ladies arrayed in tiaras and purple sashes, seated in the House of Lords and listening intently to the Queen's words. When our tentative layout was transmitted to London, squawks of outrage came back over the Telex. The guards along the parade route were not Coldstream but Grenadiers, complained the machine, and we must under no circumstances use that shot of the beautiful peeresses; one of them, an angelic creature, was just then smoldering on the hypotenuse of a particularly flagrant romantic triangle. To put her picture in the magazine at such a solemn moment, argued London, would not only insult the Queen but also bring the whole magazine into disrepute.

"Hot diggitty," said Monty Sutherland, the chief of the Legends Department, as he and several editors, male and female, pored over the slide proof. "She's the niftiest one there." Then he turned to me: "Should we run it?"

Despite the great prestige and authority of the London Bureau — it had, after all, persuaded the Palace to let us photograph the ceremony in the first place — the cringing complaint had, if anything, reinforced my desire to see the picture run.

"Of course," I replied.

"Damn right," said Sutherland. "I'll back you all the way." And he did, right up the line, but the incident made me Public Enemy No. 1 to the folks in London. When the final draft of my legends was transmitted to them, they pounced. GUARDSMEN LINING ROUTE NOT, REPEAT NOT, COLDSTREAMS BUT GRENADIERS, clicked the ticker. That was the only thing they found wrong, but the implication was that my research was suspect and not to be trusted in this or any other matter. Monty Sutherland, a journalist of the old school, cursed when he saw this cable.

"For Chrissake," he fumed, "of all the stories to screw up. Now you've got *my* ass on the line." His trust in my work had brought this upon him, and I was not happy. I collected my confidence.

"But," I replied in a subdued voice, "I don't think we did screw up. We've researched this thing up and down and those soldiers are Coldstreams. I've checked the uniforms, the numbers of buttons, and the colors of the plumes in their hats. I've even checked out their regimental histories, and checked the step-by-step evolution of those uniforms since the Battle of Waterloo."

Sutherland gazed at me in silence for a long time. He, too, had had his brushes with the omniscient London bureau. "So you say they're Coldstreams, eh?"

"Yes, sir."

"If they're not, it's your neck." There was another long silence between us. "Okay, we'll tell London they're up the creek."

By now the transatlantic exchange was arousing the interest of the magazine's higher editorial echelon. Some top editors had lightheartedly adorned their offices with prints of the prurient peeress; but now they began to follow the London cable traffic with growing concern. To the Legends Department's renewed claim that the guardsmen were Coldstreams, London — after some delay — sent back a brief and pitiless response: BUCKINGHAM PALACE CONFIRMS, REPEAT CONFIRMS, GUARDSMEN ARE GRENADIERS.

Sutherland, who as a sixteen-year-old boy had ridden across the Rio Grande with Black Jack Pershing in hot pursuit of Pancho Villa, was fit to be tied. Now the laugh was on him. He hired incompetents, and he ran a department staffed by incompetents. I knew I was dead, but as a final request asked him to review the research material I had assembled. If those bloody guardsmen were Grenadiers, then how could these photographic facts be explained? We went through it again. We sent off to every library in Washington for material that might have any bearing on British army uniforms. We checked military tailors. We called the military attaché at the British embassy. We checked histories and scores of colored drawings and diagrams. Yet all our research paled beside the confirmed word of the Palace. The Queen, of all people, must be able to identify her own soldiers, and tell one regiment from another. In a more surreal vein, we presumed she had the power to decree that the soldiers in any picture we showed her were *ipse dixit* Grenadier guardsmen. Just as the gallows humor was taking hold, a new message clicked in from London. PALACE RECHECKED PARADE MARSHAL AND SOLDIERS NOT GRENADIERS BUT COLDSTREAMS, REPEAT COLDSTREAMS. APOLOGIES. We breathed again, and I kept my job at the *National Geographic* for a while longer.

CHECKING

Many magazine editors look with disdain upon the task of checking the accuracy of manuscripts. It is, they imply, a kind of secondary skill requiring little more than an appetite for trivia and a willingness to plod in the wake of those bright lights who created the copy in the first place. My crazy caper with the Grenadiers and the Coldstreams certainly had its trivial side. One might well ask just how many readers really cared which regiment guarded Her Majesty that day. Yet to misinform those readers, even on such an insignificant matter, is surely a violation of a trust. And, if even one percent of the *Geographic*'s subscribers wrote in to complain, we would have had to contend with 60,000 righteous letters. A similar error in each of the issue's other stories could expose us to a firestorm of perhaps half a million letters each month and — if the casual attitude to truth continued — quite a number of these would have been canceling their subscriptions.

Rather than face this kind of hassle, most magazines submit all editorial material to some kind of double check. On large publications such as the *Reader's Digest* and the news magazines, a special corps of checkers is detailed to examine every word in every sentence and make sure that it is accurate. But smaller magazines cannot afford such elaborate staffing, and editors are called upon to double-check the facts in any story they are editing. You can view this as a royal pain. Or you can take a kind of madcap pride in ensuring that the facts, and only the facts, end up in your final copy. As the incident with the Coldstreams showed, the pursuit of the truth — the plain answer to the question: What *actually* happened here? — can generate an exhilaration of its own. Let's check one last book. Let's make one last phone call. As the facts become clear, the emotional reward is not unlike that experienced by the investigative reporter who, after days of sifting voter registration lists, perceives a pattern of documentable skullduggery in last month's city elections. The rewards are similar. The skills are identical.

Experienced editors develop a sixth sense for error. Their eyebrows curl into a question mark the moment they encounter an unqualified assertion. Charles Darwin was the sole articulator of the modern theory of biological evolution. John Kennedy was the youngest man ever to serve as president of the United States. Charles Lindbergh piloted the first plane to fly nonstop across the Atlantic. Sole? Youngest? First? All these assertions are, in fact, false.* Any statement that begins "All" instead of "Most" or "First" instead of "Among the first" calls for close attention and a quick move to the reference books. Sometimes editors who cannot pin something down (or are slack in their homework) employ crafty phrases to skim around the issue. Instead of saying "Ignatz is the meanest mouse in Cartoon City," they reword the sentence to read "Ignatz is one of the meanest, if not the meanest, mice in Cartoon City."

---

*The first public statement of the theory of evolution came in a joint address by Darwin and another distinguished naturalist, Alfred R. Wallace, to the Linnean Society in July 1858. The book *On the Origin of Species* appeared one year later. John Kennedy was the youngest man ever *elected* president, but Theodore Roosevelt was the youngest man ever to *serve* as president. John Alcock and Arthur Whitten-Brown flew a Vickers Vimy nonstop from Newfoundland to Ireland on June 14–15, 1919, eight years prior to Lindbergh's celebrated flight. Both were knighted.

Depending on how you unravel it, this masterpiece could be saying that Ignatz is merely one of a bad bunch, or it could be that he's the meanest of them all. Chrysler K cars are among the best-designed, if not the best-designed, autos of the decade. Red oak is one of the most efficient, if not the most efficient, wood-stove fuels available.

But if an editor is to do a good job, he or she should not be skating around the truth in this fashion. There are a number of reference works that help an editor get to the heart of the matter with a minimum of fuss. Besides the obvious good dictionary and *Roget's Thesaurus*, the following books should be on your desk, or close at hand in the magazine's library, to check facts:

Facts on File. This is a service that summarizes all events, speeches, and the like every week, and indexes them by both name and subject matter. The indexes are then summarized each quarter. Say you are editing a piece on movies. You check the index.

GLEASON, Jackie
Smokey and the Bandit II, released
8-15, 675E3

From this index entry we know that Gleason starred in the movie of that name, and that it was released 8-15, or August 15. For more details we turn to page 675, column 3, at the place marked down the page by the *E*.

An atlas. So often a story — be it about acid rain, a forest fire, a new offshore oil strike, or an accident at a nuclear plant — makes little or no sense without reference to a map. If the editor has trouble understanding the material, then a reader almost certainly will. A thumbnail map can be worth a thousand words.

BRIGHT (ACCURATE) LEADS

Sometimes a shrewd editor can liven up an otherwise routine article by building a bright new lead around an apt quotation or a weird or little-known fact. Sometimes the writer has been a few steps ahead of him on this, and it is necessary to see if the fancy footwork can be justified in fact. There are some books you should have to help you check (and get ideas for) snappy leads:

Pocket encyclopedia. Let us say you are editing a story on the resurgence of the American buffalo. The lead goes like this:

> Not since 1867, when Buffalo Bill Cody agreed to supply the workers of the Kansas Pacific Railroad with buffalo meat, has . . .

The writer is to be complimented for a snappy recap, but the editor must ask: Was it 1867? Was it the Kansas Pacific? Most desk encyclopedias can provide the answers, fast.

Brewer's Dictionary of Phrase & Fable. Some references, however, are not factual, but rooted in myth or literature. Say you are editing a piece on the California wine industry that begins

> Just as Pantagruel launched upon his immortal quest for the Holy Bottle, so . . .

Did we misspell *Pantagruel*? No. Was not the quest for the *oracle* of the Holy Bottle? Yes, and for his error the writer is compelled to stand one sizable round of chilled Chablis. Brewer's yields up authoritative information on everything from Biblical giants (Anak, Goliath, Og) to the correct name of Michael Angelo. Ready? Michelangelo Buonarroti, 1474–1564.

Bartlett's Familiar Quotations. Nothing is better calculated to cover writers' and editors' faces with scrambled egg than to show such an easy familiarity with learned authorities that one misquotes them. Here is an example from *Television/Radio Age:*

> Shakespeare didn't have public television in mind when he warned about the ideas of March.

The Bible does not say that money is the root of all evil. It declares, in fact, that "the *love* of money is the root of all evil." (Timothy I, 6:10.) Unfortunately, Ralph Waldo Emerson did not give us a stick with which to thwack the chubby posterior of every bureaucrat in town by declaring that consistency is the hobgoblin of petty minds. Instead, he offered us the lame observation that "A *foolish* consistency is the hobgoblin of *little* minds" (my italics). And I once learned the hard way that H. L. Mencken did not say "To be in love is merely to be in a state of perpetual anaesthesia." The word he used in *Prejudices* was "perceptual." So much has been written in recent years about hostages. Perhaps, for the umpteenth story on the topic, we might get a bright new lead from Francis Bacon's "he that hath wife and children hath given hostages to fortune, for they are impediments to great enterprises, either of virtue or mischief."

Guinness Book of World Records. In among the data on pie-eating contests and jampacked Volkswagens are some quite remarkable nuggets of information. You are editing a colorless, odorless, flavorless piece on inflation. Your imagination seems to have died on you, so you leaf through *Guinness* to discover that

> the world's worst inflation occurred in Hungary in June, 1946, when the 1931 gold pengo was valued at 130 trillion (1.3×10^{20}) paper pengos.

Soon a bright new lead is clicking out of your typewriter.

> Not since 1946, when the Hungarian paper pengo plunged to 130 trillionths of its equivalent in gold, has any currency taken such a beating. In the space of two months the U.S. dollar . . .

A list of additional books that can also be of great help to a magazine editor includes:

One of the annual World Fact Books, which serve as a kind of up-to-date encyclopedia.

The *U.S. Statistical Abstract* for data about how many Pennsylvanians still have outdoor johns or more than one dishwasher.

The *U.S. Government Organization Manual,* an annual publication that shows in scores of diagrams just how the federal bureaucracy comes to be in a state of administrative gridlock.

Your state's Redbook or Bluebook, showing how state government generates its own gridlock: who works for the state, what they do, and often how much they get paid.

General guides to help people get facts fast, including *The New York Times Guide to Reference Materials* by Mona McCormick and *Finding Facts Fast* by Alden Todd.

Another excellent source of information—subject to a grain of skepticism—consists of materials generated by the public relations companies and institutes that may represent the subject of your story. Doing a piece on bourbon whisky? *The Encyclopedia of Associations,* put out by the Gale Research Co., shows that the bourbon industry is represented by an outfit called the Distilled Spirits Council of the U.S., which will gladly run a huge package of information over to your office before noon. Or perhaps you plan a piece on the seeming lack of patriotism shown by the major American oil companies in recent years. Unless you tip your hand, the

American Petroleum Institute (address: 2101 L Street, N.W., Washington, D.C. 20037) will have a ton of material for you. Some of it may be self-serving. But much of it may be useful.

HEADS AND DECKS

When an editor has reworked and checked an article he or she must then compose a head and deck for it. Sometimes these terms are willfully misspelled as "hed" and "dek" to tip off the typesetter that they are not part of the story but editorial directives. In some editorial offices heads are referred to as "titles" and decks are called "subheads" or "blurbs"; the concept, however, is the same. The head consists of the words in the largest typeface. The deck, if there is one, is generally displayed in a type size lying halfway between that of the head and that of the text. Generly, the head precedes the deck on the page, but sometimes the reverse is true.

The ability to write a good head and deck is as important as the ability to get a good story idea. The task is complicated by the fact that effective heads and decks generally appeal to the reader on more than one level. The McGraw-Hill Publishing Division puts out more than forty magazines and newsletters. "Most heads," declares an in-house analysis made for some of the division's top editors,

> operate on two levels: the descriptive and the evocative. The descriptive element informs the mind in hard factual terms concerning the contents of an article. In contrast, the evocative element appeals to the emotion, the curiosity and the enthusiasm of the reader.

A purely descriptive head, the study continues, is a prosaic, colorless, rhythmless label on the story. Take the head *Closed System for Cooling Saves $1,270.* Nothing could be more specific, nor less appealing to the imagination. It does not mention cooling in vague or allusive terms; it explicitly spells out exactly what kind of cooling and exactly how much we will save, down to the nearest dollar. In contrast, the evocative head moves in the diffuse, untidy realm of the imagination. *Deadly Rain,* ran a head in an issue of *Country Journal.* The curiosity of the reader is immediately engaged. As a rule we think of rain as soft and life-giving, but this rain is different. It kills. How can that be? Where is this rain falling? What is it killing? Such questions bubble through the readers' minds, and before they know it they are into the deck.

DEADLY RAIN
Fallout from industrial pollution is destroying life that has flourished
for 250 million years.

Country Journal, November 1979

Here the magazine has combined the descriptive and evocative elements
mentioned in the McGraw-Hill study. The head evokes curiosity and concern that are then both satisfied and stimulated further by the descriptive
deck. Soon the reader is deep into the text of a piece on how the life in
the mountain lakes of the eastern seaboard is being destroyed.

Sometimes the order is reversed. The head becomes a descriptive
label and the deck carries the story's spark.

CLOSE-UP OF FOUR KEY
BATTLES FOR CONGRESS
Volatile issues, an angry electorate and well-financed opponents —
re-election is not sure thing for many incumbents this year.

U.S. News, October 13, 1980

Sometimes an evocative deck precedes a head. Here are two examples:

The Secret Fear that Keeps Us From
RAISING FREE
CHILDREN

Ms., October 1980

A rescue in this kind of weather is impossible, thought the pilot.
How long can we survive?
ORDEAL
AT HELL'S
HOLE

Reader's Digest, November 1980

TONES OF VOICE

As a rule, however, the head generally uses evocative language to arouse
the reader's interest, while the deck harnesses that aroused interest to present some basic facts to the readers. The head may make its distinctive
appeal through a simple rhyme.

CHOP

SHOPS

Police Photos of a $4 billion Racket on Stolen Car Parts

Life, August 1980

Or it may catch the reader's attention by alliteration.

FROM SURPLUS

TO SHORTAGE

OF TEENAGERS

U.S. News, November 27, 1978

But if such alliterative heads extend to more than two words, showman-ship smothers substance. The toughest of all to write involve a play on words.

The Exotic Bird:

PET OR PEST?

Parents, December 1980

Sometimes these achieve their effect by bouncing off a catch phrase, stated or unstated. One article on house insulation had the head

FIGHTING THE DRAFTS

Country Journal, November 1980

In the previous chapter we encountered a beaut:

ALTERNATIVE

LIGHT STYLES

Illumination beyond the power lines: enlightenment in the world of gas and kerosene lamps

Harrowsmith, October 1980

Effective head writing requires a sound sense of news judgment. A good head must somehow move the reader into the center of the story. But it should on no account arouse a curiosity that the content of the story can-not satisfy. Clearly, the head and deck speak to the reader in different tones of voice. When used most effectively in tandem, they can give read-ers a kind of cross-bearing to illuminate the subject matter of the story.

For best effect [the McGraw-Hill analysis continues] a deck must not tread upon the heels of the head. Rather, it must step aside and come at the story material from a different angle. The head on a story about an increase in job training schemes might read

SKILL CENTERS
DOUBLE JOB CHANCES

The deck can swing in right behind with

Employment Up More
Than 10% in States with } DECK A
New Retraining Programs

Or it might approach the story from an entirely different angle, thereby illuminating a wholly new aspect of the material with

Bank Teller Now
Head Chef at } DECK B
Resort Hotel

If this were to be represented diagrammatically, the contrasting lines of approach by Decks A and B would look as shown in figure 11.

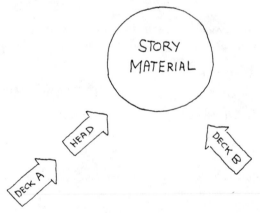

Fig. 11. Heads and decks.

By illuminating another aspect of the story Deck B substantially increases reader interest.

BREADTH THROUGH ART

The various dimensions of a complex story can be further illuminated by the use of artwork, particularly pictures. If the article on retraining programs were illuminated with a shot of a woman dance teacher and a rocket research technician, then the readers' interest would be further stimulated. In the last chapter we saw how the *New York Times Magazine* article on extended families broadened its premise by using group shots of three geographically disparate families. Though the opening anecdote concerned only one family, the artwork lent the piece instant breadth. When *Country Journal* did an article on walking sticks — entitled, simply enough, "STICKS" — the breadth of the piece was measurably enhanced by a score of portraits of famous men and women proudly sporting their sticks. An unexpectedly rakish Cal Coolidge stands next to a dreamy Sarah Bernhardt, while a skeptical Charlie Chaplin glances across at a gracefully airborne Astaire. A corpulent Oscar Wilde glowers down upon such frivolity.

This is a clear example of artwork, head, and text all working together to enhance the impact of the story upon the reader's mind. In chapter 5 we discussed leads and showed that to be effective they must somehow encapsule the essence of the story. In this chapter we have seen that this is also true of heads and decks. But we have also seen that these three must not duplicate each other. The deck must not track in upon the heels of the head, and the lead of the text must not follow in turn upon the heels of the deck; each must, in fact, approach the story topic from a different angle. This by now is a familiar principle to us. It is the *diverseness* of these three verbal pointers that arouses the reader's curiosity, that hints at paradox and makes him or her say "Hmmmm . . . how is all that possible?" Soon the reader is deep into the text, and the best editor in the world cannot do better than that.

9

EDITING 2

Fine-Tuning—Transitions,
Signposts, and Quasars

I N 1960 ASTRONOMERS in the United States and England identified some strange new radiations emanating from the depths of intergalactic space. When analyzed on the spectrograph, the incoming waves did not accord with any known chemical element in the universe, and many scientists declared that these distant pulses of energy —or quasars, as they were called—violated the ordinary laws of physics.

The astronomers vainly sought a rational explanation for these weird phenomena. After much speculation they eventually came up with a theoretical "model" that, under certain unusual conditions, was capable of manifesting the characteristics of a quasar. The parameters under which the model operated suggested that quasars were in fact galaxies-in-the-making and that the strange emissions could be explained if the sources of those emissions were moving away from the observer at great speed. One quasar was shown to be moving away from the earth at the colossal speed of 30,000 miles per second, or 16 percent of the speed of light. Then a more distant quasar was found; its spectrographic red shift showed it to be moving away at 36 percent light speed. The farther away the quasars, it seemed, the faster they moved away from our own galaxy. Since then some quasars have been spotted more than 15 billion light years distant, and escaping at 90 percent of the speed of light. Nothing has been found beyond this extraordinary limit, and astronomers have used their highly sophisticated model to conclude that these farthest quasars were alone because they rode on the very hinge of space and time, racing outward on the ultimate edge of the reality that is our universe.

If scientists can devise a model that goes a long way toward accounting for an abstruse phenomenon like the quasar, then surely it is possible — if we don't mind coming down to earth with a bump — to devise some kind of model that delineates the structure and behavior of the magazine article. I am not suggesting that we formulate some computer program into which we blindly pour our facts, and expect them to come out in the form of a personality profile or a trend. But we have discerned from the Ruark diagram and the DEE-System that there is a clear logic underlying most major story forms. Can such logic be refined into a quasarlike model that yields us insights into the fundamentals of the editorial process?

The notion of such a model is not as farfetched as it may first appear. Modern game theory provides models that effectively help business leaders and military strategists plot their next move. Why shouldn't the editor apply similar techniques to help in the task of finding the best head, deck, lead, and organizational pattern for an article? The editor may feel that this places him out there with the quasars, on the far side of reality. But a game theorist would not find the problem so exotic; indeed, the editorial tasks enumerated above can be viewed as relatively simple problems in basic search theory. After all, the problem of retrieving a replacement part from a huge warehouse inventory or the problem of searching for an enemy submarine in the depths of the Atlantic is not too different from the problem of finding the best possible headline in the oceans of words that go to make up the English language!

A rather elementary model can be devised for the "inverted pyramid" story structure used by most daily newspapers. It is mechanical in nature. In the same way that a truck mechanic strips out a faulty alternator, so a busy city editor can strip out the tail-end paragraphs he does not need without destroying the part of the story for which he has space. The thirty-paragraph story on the holdup of a bank can be cut to fifteen paragraphs, or to five paragraphs, and still make perfect sense to its readers.

The model for the inverted pyramid is one of simple succession. If A, B, C, D, E, and so forth, are paragraphs, then the rule is that the editor may only omit a paragraph if he has already omitted its successor. That is to say, he may not eliminate C if he has not already eliminated D and before that E.

If a magazine editor were to treat a well-written magazine article in this fashion, two things would happen. First, he would hear a scream from his fellow editors that the surviving paragraphs made no sense. And second, next time he went down to the Press Club for a quiet drink he'd find the author of the article threatening him with the blunt end of a pool cue.

Such an outburst does not prove that magazine writers are either more violent or more temperamental than their counterparts in the world of newspapers. They are not. But it does suggest that unlike a newspaper story, a magazine article is not a taxi line of readily expendable parts. Each component of a magazine article is related to each other component to form a coherent unity. If a part is removed it is like tearing a limb off a tree or an animal; in all probability what remains of that living thing will die. Indeed, if even a single word of a magazine article is altered, that change is likely to reverberate through the whole paragraph, and it may even place the entire article into a radically different focus. If too abrupt a change is made, that article will undoubtedly die, taking a small piece of the writer's soul with it.

TRANSITIONS

The chief difference between the mechanistically organized story (e.g., inverted pyramid) and the organically structured story (e.g., personality profile) is to be found not so much in the parts themselves as in the *relationships* between those parts. The basic raw material of facts and quotations may be the same for both kinds of story. It is the way these facts are arranged, the web of relationships between them, that is critical to the mode of organization.

Certain kinds of sentences — generally called "transitions" — are used to link various parts of a magazine article and bring them into a coherent whole. If the four organizational forms identified in the mnemonic SHIP (see chapter 3) are viewed as the bone structure of any particular magazine story, then the transitional sentence must be seen as the gristle-like tissue that holds the bones together while allowing them to flex. I use the word "sentence," but in fact a transition may be composed of a few words, a complete sentence, or an entire paragraph. Its primary function is to create a bridge that leads the readers' interest from one part of the article to another. If a transition is handled deftly, the readers will be carried from amplification to flashback, and from flashback to whither, and hardly notice it. But if it is wrongly angled or wrongly emphasized, then the readers' attention walks off into space and the article falls flat on its face.

"The ability to write a good transition," says Leonard Robinson, who served as an editor of many magazines, including the *New Yorker* and *Esquire*, before he became head of the magazine sequence at the Columbia Graduate School of Journalism, "is quite simply the difference between a $30,000-a-year editor and a $50,000-a-year editor." This quantum

jump in salary is not offered just because an editor has a dab way with
words. A transition is only as effective as the article's underlying organization. A good transition presupposes material that has already been laid
into a clear organizational pattern; it also presupposes a sensitivity on the
part of the editor to the complex web of relationships between the various
parts of that article.

Now let's take a look at some examples of good transitions and
some examples of bad transitions.

> Both women were in Washington last week to testify before a congres-
> sional committee considering legislation on "child snatching." WHILE
> THERE ARE no official statistics, it's estimated that between 25,000
> and 100,000 children are kidnapped by their own parents each year.
> BUT UNDER federal law it is not illegal for a parent to take his or her
> own child unless it can be shown that the child is in danger.
>
> Representative Charles Bennett is trying to change that. He has intro-
> duced a bill that would make it a federal crime to "snatch" a child and
> includes a clause allowing the FBI . . .
>
> *Maclean's,* July 7, 1980

Here the transitional words have been put in capital letters, and it can be
seen how they serve to adroitly move the argument into different aspects
of the story. Here is another example from an article on sports medicine:

> Some of the research has led to ingenious new methods of mending
> athletes' torn or injured bodies — including new ways to repair battered
> knees or ankles, lessen muscular pain and cope with exhaustion. The
> scientific work has also brought about the improvement of athletic
> performance through the development of sophisticated machinery
> that analyzes sports techniques — identifying strong points and flaws,
> for example — and the refinement of knowledge about how diet, hot
> weather or aging affects physical activity, and vice versa.
>
> DESPITE THESE ACCOMPLISHMENTS, the expanding field of
> sports medicine is not in a state of total harmony, There is behind-the-
> scenes arguing over who is qualified to treat patients and over which
> methods of treatment are preferable or even valid. The contention . . .
>
> *New York Times Magazine,* October 5, 1980

We see here how the upper-cased transition takes the reader's attention
and steers it into a contrary line of thought. We shall return to these three
examples of transition in a minute, but first let us examine some transitions that might be refined still further to bring out the full potential of

the material. Here is an example from a story in the *Smithsonian* about environmentalist moviemaker Hope Ryden.

> . . . before the Supreme Court. The Act's constitutionality was up-
> held and the horses' right to exist was guaranteed, at least legally.
>
> Hope Ryden was born in St. Paul, grew up in Illinois, but every sum-
> mer her family retreated to a cabin in the woods of northern Wiscon-
> sin. There were few other children for miles around the Rydens' cabin,
> so she became accustomed to spending hours in the forest alone,
> watching animals. She recalls a time when she was about nine years
> old, meeting one of the last wolves in that part of the country: "I was
> walking in the woods when all of a sudden, there it was. We looked
> at each other for a long moment. That wild animal struck a deep note
> in me."
>
> She earned her bachelor's degree at the University of Iowa, did grad-
> uate work at Columbia, and began a career in film making. She wrote,
> produced and directed some 40 films.
>
> *Smithsonian,* November 1980

Here some transitions are made conspicuous by their absence. The article moves from the incident of the horses and the Supreme Court straight into a flashback on Ms. Ryden's youth. Think how the material would have flowed if a transitional sentence like "Hope Ryden has been fighting for the rights of animals for most of her life" had been inserted before the material on her childhood. Thus alerted, readers would have found it easier to shift their attention into a new phase of the article.

There is a similar swift change in direction when the story moves from the dramatic quote about the wolf to Ryden's college career. We are left in suspense. We want to hear more about the vulpine encounter and its effects on Ryden. Instead, we skitter on to a discussion of her bachelor's degree. We are tempted to ask if the encounter had any effect on the course of her future studies. If not, then perhaps it could be profitably used elsewhere in the story. But if it did, if it made her drop art history in favor of zoology at Iowa, then this should be brought out; it would have the net effect of reinforcing the impact of both the quote about the wolf and the material on her college studies. It would, in short, have helped weave the parts of the story into an organic whole.

Here is another example of a jumbled transition, taken this time from an article in *Portfolio* on the art-event creator, Christo Javacheff.

> The mounting of such a complex and large-scale piece [a 24-mile fence
> in California], both in physical and bureaucratic terms, seems to have

confirmed something deep in Christo: proposals he has long considered which deal more directly than ever before with art in a political
framework are now moving toward realization.

Christo, IN FACT, works much like an architect, developing several
ideas at once. When one project seems feasible, the others go on the
back burner until they too can be executed.

Portfolio, September/October 1980

First, there seems to be a structural problem at the end of that initial paragraph. The experience of erecting the 24-mile-long fence may have confirmed Christo's determination to execute new proposals, but it can hardly
have confirmed the proposals themselves. The readers probably got the
gist of the writer's thought, but this kind of fogging is not congruent with
first-class writing and editing. Now consider the strange use of "in fact"
at the beginning of the next paragraph. It suggests — falsely — that putting
art in a political framework is somehow a primary activity of architects.
Once again, the fog rolls in. Much better to discard the link with politics
and just write "Christo works much like an architect."

Four Types of Transition

How can editors avoid this kind of fuzziness, and use transitions
to carry forward the clear logical line of an article's development?
Some old-style editors believe that the ability to write effective
transitions is like brains or inherited wealth, a gift from heaven. But a recent analysis of transitional usages has torn aside much of the mystique
concerning this skill. There are, researchers have found, four basic kinds
of transition, and each tends to use certain words over and over again.
The four kinds of transition are categorized according to their function
within an article as

1. Support
2. Contrast
3. Muzzle
4. Conclusion

You should also note that there is another kind of sentence that looks like
a transition, but it is in fact an attention-director, or "signpost." We shall
come back to it later in this chapter.

Table 1 gives samples of key words generally found in each type
of transition.

Table 1
TRANSITION WORDS

SUPPORT	CONTRAST	MUZZLE	CONCLUSION
Indeed	But	Despite	Thus
What is more	However	Though	Therefore
In addition	In contrast	Although	Consequently
Moreover	Yet	While	In conclusion
Not only . . .	Conversely	Regardless	Finally
but also	On the other	Contrary to	
Furthermore	hand ($1 fine)	Except	
Besides		Certainly	
Considering			
Since			
Likewise			

Note: Depending on the context, some words can be used in more than one category.

The basic function of support-type words is to sustain or enhance a line of thought that is already running in the reader's mind. If you are editing an article on the recent economic upturn, a new trend in men's clothing, or the potential for producing test-tube babies, then the use of such words as *indeed, in addition, also,* and *and* will enable you to conveniently feed yet more data to your readers without seeming to sandbag them with facts. For a straightforward example of this, take a look at the opening paragraph of the *New York Times Magazine* article on sport medicine, quoted earlier. Look how much information is packed into these two sentences, and note the effective use of the word *also* in the opening words of the second sentence. Here is another example, this time from a *Parents* magazine piece on a California businessman's intention to create baby geniuses from the sperm of Nobel Prize winners.

> Certainly the idea of discarding unwanted embryos is troubling, at the very least. INDEED, the gut reaction of some of the people I talked to about all the eugenics proposals was to label them Nazism.
>
> *Parents*, October 1980

In contrast, the contrast-type words are used to set various parts of the story in opposition to one another. An argument, perhaps, has been fully developed. Now it is time to show the other side of it with such words as *but* and *however*. A caution about the phrase *on the other hand:* if you find yourself using it you should immediately wonder if you may be boring your readers to death. The editorial writers of the *New York Times* once became so leery of this lugubrious phrase, with its hints of pomposity, that they imposed a fine of $1 on anyone who let it flop out of his typewriter. There is a fine example of a contrast transition to be found at the end of the first paragraph of the quote from *Maclean's,* above.

> . . . kidnapped by their own parents each year. BUT under federal law it is not illegal . . .

Muzzle-type transitions are more complicated. Use of such words as *although, though, while,* and *despite* enables the writer to say to the reader, "Yes, we know you have questions or doubts about this matter, but instead of getting side-tracked we want to proceed to some new aspect of the topic." The phrase temporarily muzzles the doubt of the reader by acknowledging the presence of that doubt. There are two good examples of muzzle-type transitions to be found in the first two quotations given above. In the *Maclean's* article on child snatching we had:

> legislation on "child snatching." WHILE there are no official statistics, it's estimated . . .

The effect of the muzzle word "while" is to allay our misgivings about the fact that these statistics are not official. Even if we took the minimum unofficial figure of 25,000 there is still cause for great concern. There is another example of a muzzle-type transition beginning the second paragraph of the *Times* story on sports medicine:

> . . . affects physical activity, and vice versa.
> DESPITE THESE ACCOMPLISHMENTS, the expanding field of sports medicine is not in a state of total harmony.

The reader has heard a lot of good things about developments in the field. The writer freely concedes the reader's right to optimism, but at the same time warns him or her that perfection is still far off.

A conclusion-type transition enables a writer to pull a line of reasoning or a discussion together into a single focus. Words like *thus, consequently,* and *therefore* may not occur necessarily at the end of an article, but they are effective for collecting the reader's interest and projecting it into a new line of thought. Here is an example from an article on sex therapy in *Psychology Today.*

> According to Levine, "the *immediate* effects of sex therapy were striking." Fourteen of the men managed to have a firm, lasting erection during sensate focus exercises, and those 14 had successful intercourse at

least once while they were still in treatment. BUT by the time therapy ended, Levine found, "only six were able to maintain an erection during more acts of intercourse." Only one man, Levine said, "was completely cured in the best sense of the word," meaning that he was still potent a year after treatment.

John Money, the well-known sexologist at the Johns Hopkins University School of Medicine, CONCLUDES that the Masters and Johnson approach "can easily degenerate into oversimplified sexual exercises and gymnastics."

Psychology Today, August 1980

The evidence is presented (with a contrast transition BUT built in) and then Professor Money summarizes and pins the thought down in conclusion.

A final note on transitions. Sometimes, when the logical line of an article's development is especially clear, it is possible to change gears, to move the reader's interest from one part of the story to another without the use of transition words. These blind or unspoken transitions represent the highest form of the editor's art; yet they can only be used when the underlying material has been impeccably organized. An example of such a blind transition is to be found in the last sentence of the original quote on child snatching in *Maclean's.*

. . . illegal for a parent to take his or her own child unless it can be shown that the child is in danger.

Representative Charles Bennett is trying to change that.

The last sentence could have read "BUT Rep. Bennett is trying. . . ." Or it could have read "Rep. Bennett, HOWEVER, is trying. . . ." But the logic and the thrust of the words in the sentence enable the writer to move into a contrast-type transition without the use of contrast-type words. Such transitions are far more elegant. If you as an editor find you can drop out such transition words in an article without disrupting the natural logic of the piece, then you should do so.

SIGNPOSTS

Transitions herald a change in direction; they help move the reader's attention into a new line of thought. A close examination of a well-organized magazine article, however, will reveal the presence of a number of sentences that look like transitions but in fact do not amplify or change the line of argument. Instead, they preview or "signpost" material that is to follow. Putting it another way, they give the reader a kind of verbal compass course to help him or her steer through some material that might otherwise be confusing. Here is an example.:

> Those private contributions have become the lifebood of the Met. Last year, its total budget rose to $46.6 million, and even playing to 90.6 percent capacity, the opera box office could only bring in $20.4 million. The deficit was made up by $9.9 million in other revenue and more than $14.4 million in personal, foundation, and corporate contributions — including $3 million from more than 100,000 opera buffs who gave less than $100.
>
> New York, November 3, 1980

The opening sentence "signposts" the readers into and through all the detailed financial data that follow. Without it they would be plunging around blindly in all the numbers, asking themselves, "What point is being made here? Why am I supposed to be reading this?"

While most aspiring editors acknowledge the need for major transitions in an article, they are often reluctant to signpost the smaller pieces of material. Perhaps they feel that it somehow seems to call the shot. Scientific and legal procedure, and our political tradition, require us to present the evidence before drawing a conclusion. But a signpost sentence runs counter to this approach. It requires, in effect, that we declare the prisoner guilty first and then provide the evidence to prove it. We have a built-in resistance to writing signposts. It seems undemocratic. Yet, if the reader is to know what is going on, it must be done. Here is an example from Black Enterprise:

> Even though the federal government has not fully or consistently monitored affirmative action gains, some statistics are persuasive enough to support the contention that WHITE WOMEN ARE WINNING the race into the corporate executive suite. According to the latest figures compiled by the Equal Employment Opportunity Commission (EEOC), white women increased their share of managerial positions 3.6 percentage points to 15.5 percent between 1974 and 1978, while blacks increased their share only eight-tenths of a point to 3.7 percent during the same period.
>
> Black Enterprise, September 1980

When we analyze the quote we see a muzzle-type transition in the first part of the opening statement, but this quickly leads into a very strong signpost assertion that white women are moving up faster than blacks. We may feel uneasy about making such an assertion ahead of the evidence, but we must do so if the readers are to make sense of the complicated statistics that follow.

Tennis Neck

Tennis elbow is for players. Tennis neck is for spectators who sit midcourt at Flushing Meadows or Wimbledon and swivel their heads back and forth a thousand times to follow the flight of the ball. A couple of days of this can put a fan into traction or force him to eat over his left shoulder for the rest of the season. Either way, it's unpleasant.

All too often, writers and editors, particularly when dealing with a highly controversial subject, treat their readers to a case of tennis neck. Perhaps the magazine has ordered up a piece on "Abortion: Should It or Should It Not Be Legalized?" An editor, in an effort to be scrupulously fair, might present the arguments piecemeal. First an argument in favor of legalized abortion, then an argument against, on through the story. The problem with this approach is that after a few lines of such verbal tennis, the readers begin to get confused. Soon they show signs of suffering from the editorial equivalent of tennis neck, and the point of the discourse is lost to them.

Though it may smack of prejudice, the only sensible way for the editor to get out of this fix is to signpost one side of the issue at a time. The arguments for (or against) legalized abortion must be presented as a coherent whole. Then, when the readers have absorbed this side of the controversy, they are ready to hear a coherent presentation of the opposing view. But the signpost should give a strong hint as to the structure of the article. Here is a sample phrase:

> To its supporters the case for (or against) legalized abortion seems overwhelming.

By stressing the word "supporters" rather than the public as a whole, the editor gives the readers a clear hint that there is another side to the dispute, and that we will be getting to it shortly.

INSPIRATION

We have looked at the principles that underlie the presentation of a finely tuned magazine article. If the writer and editor adhere to these principles, the story will start, move along, and make its point in a clear and straight-forward manner. But for the master craftsman such logical clarity is not enough; the material must be shaken up and made to strut and caper and dazzle the reader with the evocation of unsuspected nuance. The writer becomes poet as much as craftsman and the script — by application of imagination, inspiration, hunch, intuition — is made to illuminate resonances of meaning that had not been apparent to the reader before. Here is Norman Mailer describing the start of the chaotic march on the Pentagon in *The Armies of the Night:*

> Picture then this mass, bored for hours by speeches, now elated at the beginning of the March, now made irritable by delay, now com-pressed, all old latent pips of claustrophobia popping out of the crush, and picture them as they stepped out toward the bridge, monitors in the lead, hollow square behind, next the line of notables with tens, then hundreds of lines squeezing up behind, helicopters overhead, police gunning motorcycles, cameras spinning their gears like the winging of horseflies, TV cars bursting seams with hysterically over-worked technicians, sun beating overhead — this huge avalanche of people rumbled forward thirty feet and came to a stop in disorder, the lines behind breaking and warping and melding into themselves to make a crowd not a parade, and some jam-up at the front, just what no one knew, now they were moving again. Forty more feet. They stopped. At this rate it would take six hours to reach the Pentagon [p. 108].

A journalist can describe the events of that day 'objectively' in terms of statistics — acres of grass flattened, speeches delivered, arrests made — but Mailer's evocation of this great groping column of idealists, packed tight enough to pop the "pips of claustrophobia," offers an immediacy and a level of poetic truth unattainable by conventional modes of journalism. This extra dimension is apparent in Tom Wolfe's description in *The Right Stuff* of a Navy fighter weighing 25 tons and traveling at 135 knots land-ing on the pitching deck of a carrier:

> As the aircraft came closer and the carrier heaved on into the waves and the plane's speed did not diminish and the deck did not grow steady — indeed, it pitched up and down five or ten feet per greasy heave — one experienced a neural alarm that no lecture could have prepared him for: This is not an *airplane* coming toward me, it is a brick with some poor sonofabitch riding it *(someone much like my-self!)* and it is not *gliding*, it is *falling*, a fifty-thousand-pound brick, headed not for a stripe on the deck but for *me* — and with a horrible

smash! it hits the skillet, and with a blur of momentum as big as a
freight train's it hurtles toward the far end of the deck . . . [p. 27].

Such events happen daily, but until we have read of Wolfe's flying bricks
and the blurred momentum of a freight train we landlubbers have little
or no understanding of the great human and mechanical stresses in play
on the deck of an aircraft carrier. Mailer and Wolfe clearly intend to evoke
a certain mood in the reader. But sometimes the merits of a writer's gift
lie far beyond his or her conscious intention. The celebrated lines:

> When Adam delved and Eve span,
> Who was then the gentleman?

were sung and chanted again and again by English peasants in their revolt
of 1381. Yet the words are derived from a poem by Richard de Hampole
(1290–1349) that he had intended to be a joyous hymn to the natural an-
archy of sexual love. Richard Hampole, like many good poets, wrote better than he knew.

How can aspiring writers and editors haul their material into the
magnetic field of poetic metaphor? It is not too helpful to say: Write like
Mailer! Write like Hampole! But at the very least we can acknowledge
that the possibility is there. And if inspiration should come your way,
don't repudiate it; use the poet's pen to give airy nothings a local habita-
tion and a name.

THE UNCONSCIOUS

In recent years psychologists and game theorists alike have made careful
studies of the strange phenomenon we refer to as "hunch" or "inspiration."
In many instances what was originally described as some intuitive form
of perception has turned out to be little more than the unconscious application of well-learned principles. At first glance, an extrasensory intuitive component seems to be at work at the highest levels of most major
professions. A brilliant doctor may simply glance at a patient and correctly diagnose a rare disease. A top-flight trial attorney may develop a
sixth sense for the detection of fabricated testimony. Veteran escort commanders on the North Atlantic convoys could alert their ships to the
presence of a lurking submarine before there was any reading on the electronic detection gear. And even scientists are capable of having the same
kind of experiences, as when two astronomers at Cal Tech, Jesse Green-

stein and Maarten Schmidt, finally discerned the correct explanation for
the strange quasar transmissions:

> Then a curious thing happened. Greenstein, who had studied the
> spectrum of 3C48 at length while developing his hypothesis that it
> was a star, felt that a vault door deep in his mind had swung open,
> revealing a chamber of the unconscious in which the red shift prob-
> lem had already been solved without his consciously knowing it.
>
> "Thirty-seven per cent," he said.
>
> "What?" They had been talking about 16 per cent, the red shift of the
> spectrum in front of them.
>
> "3C48!" In his mind's eye Greenstein could see the spectrum, suddenly
> rendered coherent. "Thirty-seven per cent," he said to Schmidt, who
> was looking at him a bit oddly.
>
> The two men went down the hall to Greenstein's office, took out the
> 3C48 spectrum from the files, and measured the displacement of the
> lines. It was 37 per cent. The quasar, apparently, was nearly 4 billion
> light-years distant.
>
> Looking back over the incident, Greenstein, a collector of Buddhist
> art with an interest in Oriental philosophy, said, "I have no belief in
> any mystic philosophy, but I have a great belief in the power of the
> unconscious."
>
> Timothy Ferris, *The Red Limit*, pp. 185–86

The opening of such a vault door can hardly be an act of will. The unconscious adamantly resists recruitment to the conscious purposes of the
mind. But if individuals — whether they are writers, doctors, sub-hunters,
lawyers, or scientists — acquire a profound working knowledge of the principles of their professions, then the dark tides of the unconscious may flow
their way, and offer them a surprising new mode of perception.

10

MAGAZINE PRODUCTION
Ideas into Print

Tom Rawls, the managing editor of *Country Journal*, is sitting in his office on the second floor of an eighteenth-century tavern in Manchester, Vermont. It is now the third week in January and though the sun shines brightly off the pine-clad hills nearby, the temperature hovers in the low teens and snow is piled 3 feet high against the building's clapboard wall. Deep winter in Vermont. Rawls cannot wait to join his wife and trek up into the woods behind their home; the previous evening they believe they spotted a rare species of owl, and they are anxious to confirm the identification. But just now Rawls has other business. On the desk in front of him sits a single sheet of paper that looks like a long laundry list of dates, running from December 15 through March 31 (see fig. 13). It is the schedule for the *Journal*'s April issue. Most of the articles that will go to make up that issue were chosen back in November (see chapter 3). Now the dates on the schedule tell Rawls of the thirty-odd deadlines that must be met if that issue is to become a reality. The list covers a period of three and a half months, from the initial gathering of cover possibilities before Christmas, through the whole process of production from the editing of copy, the composition of heads and decks, the designing of the artwork, the laying out and dummying of the issue, the pasting up of printed copy, the shooting and printing of final negatives, the printing and, finally, the distribution of the new issue to readers by April 1.

According to the schedule all edited copy should be off to the typesetter in New Hampshire by January 26. Yet the final revision of a story on the planting of an apple orchard has not been received back from the

Fig. 12. Managing editor at work.

author. Perhaps the heavy snows have delayed its return. Though he is hopeful it will appear in the mail tomorrow, Rawls has quietly begun to cast about for a replacement if it does not. Is there a piece, he wonders, that can be pulled from May or June? The problem, of course, is that such a last-minute move will have a nasty domino effect on succeeding issues of the magazine.

Rawls reviews the April schedule once again. "This may look simple," he tells a visitor, with a grin. "But it isn't." The form, in truth, resembles the flight plan for a 747 jet on a trip to Bombay via Capetown and Frankfurt. There'd be no problem in any of this, explains Rawls, if *Country Journal* put out only three magazines a year. "Finish one, then start another. But in fact we put out an issue every month, and that means that at any one time we are working on three and maybe even four issues at the same time."

Each schedule passes a particular issue through three basic phases of activity. These phases run four-four-six weeks in duration (see table 2). At this moment Rawls, editor-in-chief Dick Ketchum, art director Tom Morley, and other staff members are moving the April issue from phase 1 to phase 2. In the same week the editors and art director must select a cover for the May issue, and push its copy and artwork into the processing of phase 1. As they do this, they must also be bolting the March issue into its ultimate form in phase 3, and nursing the February issue through its final birth pangs before distribution a week or so from now.

"It's easy for magazine editors to get disoriented," comments Dick Ketchum dryly. "In here we are working on articles about spring and summer and when we walk out the door to go home we bump into a bank of snow."

As can be seen from figure 13, the first official event in the gestation of the April issue occurred on December 15 when the art director assembled all the color transparencies associated with the planned stories. But in reality the process of conceiving, commissioning, and reworking

Table 2
PHASES OF ACTIVITY

Phase		Time Lapse (in weeks)
1:	Processing of raw copy and artwork by magazine staffers culminating in transmission of copy to typesetter and pictures for separation and conversion.	4
2:	Preparing returned material, now in proof form, to fit space available — a function of the amount of advertising sold.	4
3:	Dispatch of finished material for photoprocessing, plate up, printing, and distribution of magazine.	6

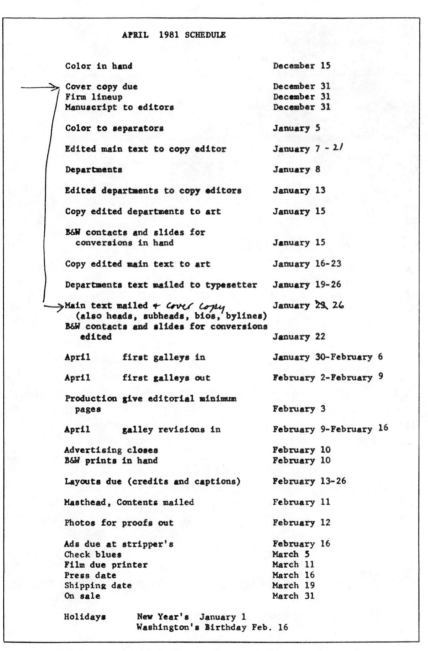

APRIL 1981 SCHEDULE

Color in hand	December 15
Cover copy due	December 31
Firm lineup	December 31
Manuscript to editors	December 31
Color to separators	January 5
Edited main text to copy editor	January 7 - 2/
Departments	January 8
Edited departments to copy editors	January 13
Copy edited departments to art	January 15
B&W contacts and slides for conversions in hand	January 15
Copy edited main text to art	January 16-23
Departments text mailed to typesetter	January 19-26
Main text mailed + *cover copy* (also heads, subheads, bios, bylines)	January 23, 26
B&W contacts and slides for conversions edited	January 22
April first galleys in	January 30-February 6
April first galleys out	February 2-February 9
Production give editorial minimum pages	February 3
April galley revisions in	February 9-February 16
Advertising closes	February 10
B&W prints in hand	February 10
Layouts due (credits and captions)	February 13-26
Masthead, Contents mailed	February 11
Photos for proofs out	February 12
Ads due at stripper's	February 16
Check blues	March 5
Film due printer	March 11
Press date	March 16
Shipping date	March 19
On sale	March 31
Holidays New Year's January 1	
Washington's Birthday Feb. 16	

Fig. 13. Publishing schedule for an issue of *Country Journal.*

Fig. 14. Dick Ketchum and Tom Morley, art director of *Country Journal*, confer on the selection of a cover picture for the April issue. They chose a painting of an apple called a Seek-No-Further.

those articles has been going on for months before that date. Once the art director has the color slides "in-house" he will sit down with Ketchum and picture editor John Wood and determine which picture could best go on the magazine's cover. The decision is an important one, for it will in large part determine the public response to the April issue on the news-stands. The picture should have a clear focal point (a single animal, rather than a gaggle of them; one face, rather than a crowd) and the visual back-ground should be of consistent texture to permit "showcasing" of article titles on the cover. If this background moves from snow to deep shadow, or from dark trees to sunlit rock, the titles are apt to be lost in contrasts. For the April cover they select a beautiful painting of a huge rosy apple that is known to horticulturalists as a Westfield Seek-No-Further. It has been culled from the article on old-time apples. "We could have gone with the kingfisher," commented Rawls, "but we'd just had too many animal covers in recent issues."

Within a day or so the same group reassembles with the addition of Tom Rawls and associate editor Jake Chapline and determines what will go into the preliminary lineup of articles (see fig. 15). This consists of nine regular columns of predictable length, plus a basic core of articles iden-tified as follows:

Preliminary December 15, 1980

COUNTRY JOURNAL

April 1981

Approx. Length

LAUNDROMAT - Bachman   2,000

PONDS - Cook   5,280

GARDEN PATHS - Doherty   1,000

GREENING OF THE SOUTH BRONX - Hand   2,500

HOW GOOD WERE THE OLD-TIME APPLES? - Hill   4,400
     Sidebars

KINGFISHER - Laycock   3,400

PEGGIE AND CARL TCHERNEY - Meyer   2,200

PLANTING ORCHARD - *Hill*

WHITE BIRCH - Flint   887

HERRING COVE (poem) - Huntington (galleys)

Cumberland Gen'l Store - Flanagan (galleys)

DEPARTMENTS

BOX 870

LETTER FROM THE COUNTRY

VEGETABLE GARDEN

ALMANAC

COOK'S TOUR

READERS' COUNTRY

LISTENER

OUT OF THE ATTIC

WHAT'S AHEAD

Departments - January 16 - 26
Main text - January 23

Fig. 15. Preliminary lineup of articles.

"Garden Paths"—a short how-to piece for the home gardener showing how he or she can increase fertility by relocating paths every year or two.

"Greening of the South Bronx"—a human interest "issue" piece on how a successful vegetable co-op works in the Bronx.

"How Good Were the Old-Time Apples?"—a 4,400-word cover story with lavish illustrations of how the apple looked to painters of the past.

"Planting an Apple Orchard"—a piece telling readers how to recreate some of the sights of the previous piece in their own back yards.

"Kingfisher"—a long, informative natural history piece.

"Peggy and Carl Tcherney"—a personality profile on some expert manuscript illuminators; it is illustrated with beautiful examples of the subjects' work.

Additional articles are then built onto this basic core; a piece on ponds, a short essay on the laundromat, a piece on the white birch, and a poem.

The arrangement of articles within a magazine differs from one publication to another. Some—like the *New York Times Magazine*—prefer to "showcase" their articles, beginning them all in the first few pages of the book, and then jumping them back. Others—like the news magazines—prefer a "read-through" approach that has the reader complete one story before encountering the next. Though Ketchum's *Country Journal* showcases several top articles together on the cover, it is textually organized in a read-through format. "We strive to open with a well-written general-interest piece," says Tom Rawls. "Then we may follow this with a couple of how-tos, or maybe a good profile." These are followed by a major four-color story that crosses the book's main centerfold, or gutter.

"When people pick up a magazine," Rawls says, "they tend to flip it open at the staple, and we like to catch their attention with some really dramatic artwork." In the previous December issue the editors used this center space for a beautiful color spread on life in a Greek Orthodox monastery located in New York's Taconic Mountains. The February issue ran a subtly colored piece on how to stencil your own wallpaper. These center-pieces in *Country Journal* are generally followed by articles of more specialized appeal, and longer stories that the editors like to jump through the back-of-the-book advertising.

As the April issue is readied for publication, the articles are lined up as follows in order of appearance:

1. Old-Time Apples—opening spread

2. Planting an Apple Orchard

3. Tcherney Illuminations—centerfold

4. Kingfisher

5. Essay on Laundromat

6. Greening of S. Bronx

7. Ponds: How to Build One

8. Garden Paths

Unforeseen circumstances, however, have a way of changing the official lineup. The story on ponds is a strong service piece that tells the reader step by step how to make a farm pond that won't drain out or silt up into a marsh. But, as one staff member points out, trying to dig a pond amid the showers of April would simply invite readers to create a quagmire. So, scratch ponds for April, and bounce it to July or August. As a substitute, the editors wheel in a neatly diagrammed article on old wooden jackplanes, how they work and how to use them.

The story on ponds is not the only problem to confront the editors in the April line up. The lead article contains no fewer than thirty-three paintings (thirty-four, with the Westfield Seek-No-Further on the cover) of various old-time apples. All this fruity portraiture, however, will be running just one story away from the profile of the Tcherneys, with their illuminated manuscripts. "Tcherneys is a great story," remarks Rawls. "At first we tried moving it back, and putting the kingfisher piece across the centerfold." But there were still problems. After quite a bit of discussion the editors realized it was not the Tcherney artwork in itself that caused the clash. "It was more the *kind* of artwork," explained *Country Journal*'s managing editor. "Both the old-time applepiece and the Tcherney piece are illustrated not with photos, or diagrams, but with beautiful paintings." For this reason the Tcherney profile was moved ahead a month or two, and an article on the Cumberland General Store put in its place. This store, located in Tennessee, is one of special interest to readers because it specializes in stocking every tool that a small farmer or rural homesteader could possibly need. The results of this rearrangement are promulgated in the revised lineup of January 6 (see fig. 16). The presentation of articles in order of appearance now becomes:

1. Old-Time Apples — opening spread

2. Planting an Apple Orchard

3. Kingfisher — centerfold

4. Essay on Laundromat

5. Greening of S. Bronx

6. Planes

Revised January 6, 1981

COUNTRY JOURNAL
April 1981

Approx. Length

LAUNDROMAT - Bachman   2,000

GARDEN PATHS - Doherty   1,000

CUMBERLAND GENERAL STORE - Flanagan (galleys)   3,948

GREENING OF THE SOUTH BRONX - Hand   2,500

HOW GOOD WERE THE OLD-TIME APPLES? - Hill   4,400
    Sidebars

KINGFISHER - Laycock   3,400

~~PEGGIE AND CARL TCHERNEY - Meyer~~   ~~2,200~~

PLANTING ORCHARD

PLANES - Watson   1,782 & drawings

WHITE BIRCH - Flint   887

HERRING COVE (poem) - Huntington (galleys)

DEPARTMENTS

BOX 870

LETTER FROM THE COUNTRY

VEGETABLE GARDEN

ALMANAC

COOK'S TOUR

READERS' COUNTRY

LISTENER

OUT OF THE ATTIC

WHAT'S AHEAD

Departments - January 16 - 26
Main text - January 23

Fig. 16. Revised lineup of articles.

7. Cumberland Store

8. Garden Paths

Generally an issue will run between 96 and 132 pages, depending upon the number of advertising pages sold. The formula for computing the amount of editorial material required is a rather complicated one. For issues up to 100 pages, the editorial and advertising is split on a ratio of 60:40 respectively. Additional pages can be stitched in minimum increments of four, and such increments are generally split 50:50 between editorial and ads. In each issue regular columns take up some 16 to 17 pages of copy, leaving a gap of between 40 and 51 pages available for main text and illustration.

Country Journal's editors will have no precise reckoning on the number of editorial pages to be filled in the April issue until after a meeting between the Journal's publisher and his production and advertising directors on February 10. But, the editors do know that last year's April issue ran 104 pages, comprising 42 pages of ads and 62 pages of editorial material. This means that, without the columns, they were required to fill a space of 46 pages of text.

Working from the revised lineup, Rawls and Chapline now process the selected manuscripts through their final edit. When all editing is completed, managing editor Rawls writes the heads and decks for each article and then passes them along to Dick Ketchum, who will alter or fine-tune each piece to his liking. As this is being done, picture editor John Wood is dispatching all color pictures to Washington, D.C., or New York (where they will be sent to special studios in Switzerland and Italy) for separation. This is a delicate process in which four separate negatives are made, one each for the four colors — magenta, yellow, cyan blue, and black — used in the final printing. To separate magenta a greenish filter, which deters yellow and blue, is placed over the picture before it is recorded on film. The yellow component is shot through a violet filter (deterring red and blue), and the blue component is shot through an orange filter (deterring yellow and magenta). The black component is reproduced by use of a filter that masks out all primary colors. The separation negatives are then carefully checked to ensure that the variously imaged layers overlay each other with the utmost precision.

Back in the Journal's editorial offices in Manchester, the copy for the main text and departments is being passed in a steady stream from the editors to copy editors Ann Landi and Friede Harris, who check for spelling, grammar, and factual error. If the copy is very messy, it will be retyped. The manuscript is then sent to art director Tom Morley, who will mark in typefaces for heads, decks, and copy and then send it through the mails to the magazine's typesetter in Lebanon, N.H. Morley retains a photocopy of the text to help him plan his artwork.

Maintaining a steady flow of work for all hands is a major concern for the managing editor of almost every magazine in existence. But the unpredictable nature of the process always presents a problem, and the *Country Journal* is no exception. Rawls had been concerned about a delay in receiving the revised manuscript on the apple orchard story; it finally arrived just one day before it was due to be dispatched to the typesetter. Having got most of the other stories neatly tucked up, Rawls is able to push it through on the run. "We strive for a steady flow, but in reality the process is sometimes like a pig going through a boa constrictor," concedes Rawls. "Things get backed up and then digested in one great lump." Like every other managing editor, he is constantly making adjustments in an effort to achieve a smoother traffic flow.

Before the shooting copy, or "repros," returns from the typesetter, Ketchum, Rawls, and Chapline use the time to chivy forward the work on the issues that precede and succeed the April issue. They may also handle long-term correspondence with authors preparing articles for succeeding editions. In the art department, Tom Morley and assistant art director Bill Suplee are preparing black-and-white pictures and figuring out how each article can best be laid out with its artwork.

COLD TYPE

At the Whitman Press in New Hampshire a keypunch operator, working at a VIP Mergenthaler System, sets the main text in 10-point Electra, and heads and decks on a display type machine in Goudy or variations of Goudy typeface (see fig. 17). In the last decade the technology of typesetting and printing has been revolutionized by the use of computerized "cold-type" composing systems. No longer do spidery linotype machines stamp out flat nuggets of molten type; instead, an operator punches the letters and words of a manuscript onto a lettered keyboard that is attached to a desk-sized box. This system works like a giant in-house typewriter. The keyboard signals electronically reproduce and imprint the words in black type on white proofsheets (or repros) in the line length and typeface specified by the art director. "In simple, comparative terms," declares Professor Mario R. Garcia, author of *Contemporary Newspaper Design*, "cold type is cheaper than hot type, and cleaner. Also, because everything that can

Fig. 17. VIP Mergenthaler typesetter enables one operator to set entire text of *Country Journal* in some 20 hours of work at the keyboard. Courtesy, Whitman Press, Inc., Lebanon, N.H.

be photographed can be reproduced, it offers greater design possibilities and creates greater availability of typefaces — both the readable and the not-so-readable."

As they emerge from the typesetting machine, the repros are duplicated. The originals are then dispatched to production manager Bill Farnham at the *Country Journal*'s business office in Brattleboro, while the photocopies of the columns of set type are returned to Tom Morley in Manchester. The standard column width for the *Journal* is 13 picas, or 2 1/6 inches. Now it is possible to determine exactly how much column space each article will occupy, together with its head, deck, and artwork. Sometimes this copyfitting does not work out precisely and type will overrun the space alloted to it. As a rule, however, *Country Journal* lets its stories run their full length and then builds the artwork — containing more or less white space — around it. Other magazines generally specify a maximum line length for an article and it is sometimes necessary to cut five, ten, or even fifty lines out of a piece before it will fit snugly into the layout.

COPYFITTING

Over the years editors have developed a number of tricks to make the task of cutting and copyfitting as painless as possible. Perhaps a whole paragraph can be dropped out, though this is difficult if the article is organized into an organic whole. Another way to cut lines without cutting too much copy is to slice away at the widows (the incomplete lines) at the end of each paragraph. If there are thirty paragraphs in the article, then an adroit editor can pick up thirty lines of copy for the loss, say, of only ten lines of text. For obvious reasons editors strive to make cuts at the end, rather than at the beginning of paragraphs; that way, the typesetter only has to reset one or two lines, instead of an entire paragraph.

On February 3 *Journal* publisher William Blair meets with production manager Farnham and advertising manager Steven Lembke in the magazine's Brattleboro offices and determines that on the basis of current ad sales the optimum size for April would be an issue of 104 pages, the same as last year. For Dick Ketchum, under the ad/edit formula outlined above, this means that he must be prepared to provide a maximum of 62 pages of editorial material; in fact, however, this is likely to be somewhat less, depending upon final ad sales. At this point Ketchum, Rawls, and Morley dope out an issue column count (see fig. 18), which outlines how much space, computed in columns, each story is likely to occupy. A glance at the top left corner of the form shows the computation for the reader features amounting to 52 columns, on 17 pages plus one column. When these 52 columns are combined with the 55 columns (lower right) of the shorter articles, they produce a total of 107 columns, or 36 pages. This must in turn be added to the 28 pages taken up by the major articles — making a grand total of 64 pages.

The editors know that this exceeds the space available in the April issue, and that it must be pruned back. On February 10 advertising sales close and they are told over the phone that a total of 137½ columns, or nearly 46 pages, of ads have been sold and that they now have to fit their editorial copy and artwork into a little under 59 pages. The juggling begins. Some of Rawls' and Morley's calculations can be seen in the lower right margins of the column count. To bring in the issue at 59 pages, the space occupied by the shorter stories and the regular feature must be cut from 36 to 30 pages. Two sticks of type are pruned out of the Listener column (top left — it goes from 9 to 7), though this is offset by a one-column increase in book reviews (entitled "Readers" on the form). The edit is still much too tight, and it is decided to drop the entire article on white birch trees.

Columns

Contents & Masthead		4	
Box 870	10+30	11½	
Letters	3+35	5	(4½)
Veg Garden	3+9	3½	
Almanac	3+57	4½	26
Cook's	3+35	6	
Readers'	4+49	✗	6
Listener/~~Craft~~ 3+43		✗	7
What's Ahead / Attic		4	

month...... APRIL '81

COLUMNS...................................

	52/ .741	title & text	color	b/w photo	drawgs	side bars	misc	Total cols	Total pages
TOTAL									
Garden Paths	2+43	3			3			(5)	2
Kingfisher	7+42	(+) 8	5	? (2)				13	(5)
Old Time Apples	4+20	5	15			R+2 D0+26			10
Planting Orchard	7+18	8	1½		4(5) 3 MAP	1+3C D0+36			6
Greening of Bronx	7+5	(+) 7½	7½	? 2½					6
Cumberland General Store 6+45		(+) 7	5-8						4
Planes	4+49	(+) 5			9			14	(5)
Laundromat	4+18	5	1-2					7	(2-1/4)
White Birch	1+64	2			2			4	
Herring Cove	0+31x2							(+) 1	
								55	28
								52	30
							3)107	36	
					39 / 52				(59)
					3)91				
					30+1				

Fig. 18. Issue column count.

Once the edit is pretty much aligned with the space available, Tom Morley assembles the pagination breakdown (see fig. 19), which specifies with precision how each page of the issue will be used. Page numbers run down the left and up the right margin because the cross-referenced

APRIL   2/11

#						#
1		(3)			3 ATTIC	104
2	MASTHEAD 1	2	3			103
3	CONTENTS 3		3			102
4	BOX 870 1	2	3			101
5		(3)	3			100
6	1	2	3 Classified	(AHEAD)		99
7		(3)	1	2 PO-FM		98
8	1	2	2	1		97
9	Dutch (3)	2	1			96
10	2	(1)	2	1		95
11	1½	1½	1	2 READER'S		94
12	1	2	2	1		93
13		(3)	2	1		92
14	1	2	1	2		91
15	1	Sears (2)	2	1		90
16	1	2	3 House			89
17		House 3	1	2 LISTENER		88
18	1	2	1	2		87
19		3		3 PATHS		86
20	RMK 3		3			85
21	2		1	3 Bookshelf		84
22	ALMANAC 1	2	1	2		83
23		3	2	1		82
24	1	2		3		81
25		3		3		80
26	1	2		3		79
27	1½	1½		3 CUMBERLAND		78
28	COOK'S 3		3 C.P.S			77
29	1	2	2	1		76
30	2	1	1	2		75
31		3	1	2		74
32	GARDEN 1	2	1	2		73
33		3	1	2		72
34	1	2		3		71
35	1½	1½		3 PLANES		70
36	APPLES		2 (HOLD)	1		69
37			2	1		68
38			1	2		67
39			1	2		66
40						65
41						64
42						63
43				GREENING		62
44			2	1		61
45			2	1		60
46	ORCHARD			3		59
47				3 LAUNDROMAT		58
48			2	1		57
49			2	1		56
50						55
51						54
52	KINGFISHER					53

Fig. 19. Pagination breakdown.

pages are physically connected to each other; that is to say, pages 1 and 2 are to be printed on the same piece of paper as pages 103 and 104. The figures down the centerline of the breakout represent the column space of the advertisements on each page, and the figures down the left and right outer margins indicate the columns of editorial copy. Thus, page 4 is composed of one column of readers' letters (titled "Box 870") and two columns of advertising. The short lateral dashes across the page number show the beginning of a new signature (sheets of paper folded as one unit) which, according to printing arrangements, may run 4, 8, 16, or a maximum of 32 pages. Not all signatures are available for color printing, and so Morley must arrange the artwork of the story so it falls into an appropriate signature. In this issue of *Country Journal* the center signatures, running from page 37 to page 68, will be in four color so that the stories (Old-Time Apples, Orchards, Kingfishers, and Bronx) that require the full treatment must be located here. The first two signatures of the magazine — that is, pages to 1 to 16 and 89 to 104 — will be capable of carrying two colors.

With the pagination breakout set, Tom Morley and Bill Suplee can now put the finishing touches on the layout for each article. The duplicated repros, head type, and proofs of artwork are pasted onto full-sized layout sheets, which are then sent over the mountains to production manager Bill Farnham in Brattleboro. When he receives this material, Farnham takes it, together with the original repro copy received from the typesetter, down to the studios of Bristol Offset in Brattleboro. Here it is pasted with great precision onto each page in the configuration stipulated by Tom Morley's galleys (see fig. 20).

When Bristol's paste-ups are complete, they are checked and pronounced camera-ready. Each page is then photographed using a Kodak System camera and processors. The resulting "final negatives" are then dispatched to an out-of-state printer, where they are converted to cylindrical plates and put on Webb offset presses, and run off on 50-lb Pubtex paper. The signatures are then assembled, bound, and labeled with subscribers' names and addresses. This final step, with its assessment of mailing dues, is checked and approved by an employee of the U.S. Post Office who works full-time in the printing plant.

The paste-up and processing of camera-ready copy at Bristol Offset generally takes some two weeks. Printing, binding, and addressing the magazines takes about four days, enabling the April issue of the *Journal* to be ready for shipment by March 18. Two days later Blair & Ketchum's loyal subscribers are leafing through the pages of their new magazine and reading about the miraculous kingfisher, the good old-time apples of yesterday, and how to start their own apple orchard (see fig. 23). As they

Fig. 20. Precise right-angle cuts are made on Trimark machine by Ruth Bristol so that *Country Journal* copy and ad pages can be pasted up square. Photo by W. Allan Gill.

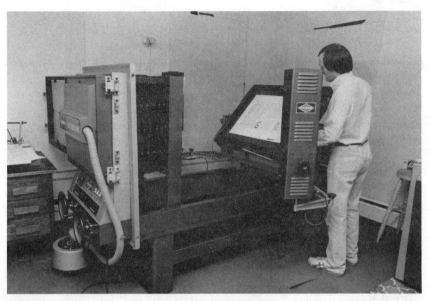

Fig. 21. Offset camera shoots four pages at a time from *Country Journal's* pasted-up columns. Photo by W. Allan Gill.

complete this last story, they may glance out at their back acreage and ponder if they might not take the author's advice and start their own orchard, little knowing that the article it just took them 20 minutes to read has been in a process of intensive preparation for more than half a year.

Country Journal's production process is complicated by the fact that it farms out the tasks to small firms in several different cities. In recent years more and more publications are buying or renting the equipment that enables them to set cold type right in their own offices. This "in-house" typesetting gives them great control over their own operation and, in a typical case, can cut lag-time between final deadline and distribution of the printed magazine from three weeks to one week.

The *Journal* has a one-week turnaround time between dispatching manuscript and receiving repros for galleys. The seven publications in the Magazines For Industry chain (747 Third Ave., New York, N.Y. 10017) have a two-day turnaround from their in-house Compugraphic typesetter. But in an emergency, the process can work even faster than that.

"I can give a late-breaking story to the typesetter at 9:00 A.M. and

Fig. 22. Page negative receives final check from Gordon Bristol. Any defects or chinks of light are painted, or "opaqued," out of the film before it is dispatched to the printer. Photo by W. Allan Gill.

Fig. 23. Cover and interior of April 1981 *Country Journal.*

get corrected galley copy back by 10:30 A.M.," declares Bob Benchley, managing editor of MFI's flagship publication *Food & Drug Packaging* (circulation 55,000). "If the photos or other artwork and heads are ready to go with it, I can run it into the art department and have a camera-ready mechanical back, ready to go to the printer, by the end of the afternoon. Total time elapsed — eight hours."

Larger magazines have correspondingly more sophisticated equipment made by such firms as IBM and Mergenthaler. With the Atex System installed at *U.S. News,* the writer composes his or her story right on the video display terminal (VDT). A computer automatically ensures that it is correctly hyphenated and then stores it in columns of specified line length. On command, the story will appear on an editor's VDT, where any appropriate changes can be made. Artwork, previously inserted into another computer by electronic scanner, can then be married up with the edited copy to produce page layouts. Magnetic tapes of these layouts can then punch out final page proofs that, when corrected, can be transmitted to the magazine's various printing plants.

Nearly all major magazines employ equipment of similar or even greater sophistication, so that a story that used to take one hour to place in type can now be processed in less than 3 minutes. Some systems use OCR-related typewriters (OCR stands for Optical Character Recognition), which eliminate the keypunch operator; the machine simply reads the reporter's or writer's copy off the typed page and sets it in print. Today top editors don't even have to leave their elegant estates in Connecticut, or their haciendas on the beaches of Baja; by just throwing a switch on their home computer terminal they can dial up any story in the upcoming book and make any editorial changes they wish.

Technology once available only to the largest publications is now filtering down to publishers of the smallest magazines and newsletters. Some of the high-tech terminology, however, can be quite misleading. "Desktop publishing" (or DTP as it's sometimes called) suggests that aspiring publishers can — for an investment of about $10,000 — acquire a keyboard and a set of buff-colored boxes that will enable them to write, print, and distribute the magazine of their dreams, all without leaving their kitchen. "Desktop publishing" is, of course, a misnomer; what it really should be called is "desktop editing, typesetting and layout." The process, when it is functioning properly, enables the publisher to edit completed copy of the writer, set it in a selected typeface at desired column widths and then, working on screen with a "mouse" or similar indicator, marry it up and lay it out with appropriate graphic materials. The resulting pages are then passed through a high-quality laser printer (with a resolution of at least 1,270 dots per inch) to yield up camera-ready copy. The task of printing up thousands of copies of every page, and then binding and distributing them, takes place in the customary fashion.

Today, most publishers acknowledge that even technology of the highest sophistication must still contend with two irreducible processes fundamental to any editorial production. These are:

1. *Creation:* The process of experiencing and organizing facts, feelings, ideas, and judgments in an ordered sequence of verbal and visual constructs.

2. *Dissemination:* The process of presenting those symbols or constructs in understandable form to a large number of people.

Today, the rapidly evolving technology addresses itself primarily to the task of smoothing away the problems of dissemination. How can we develop a delivery system that is swifter, cheaper, and more accurate? Similarly, such technology may assist the process of creation. But it can also warp it out of shape. Perhaps a competent writer can compose an inverted-pyramid news item directly on a video display terminal. But can he or she really do justice to a more complicated article by writing it in this fashion? Similarly, can we expect an editor to rearrange the pieces of a long article when he or she can only glimpse a part of it at any one time on the terminal? To be sure, some kind of job can be lashed together; but is it the best job, the one that the topic and the readership deserve? It is hoped that publishers and production managers will realize that new technology, while demonstrably faster, cleaner, and cheaper, may impose an increasingly stiff price upon the quality of the editorial product.

11

THE SLEEPING BEAUTY OF LANGUAGE

NOT LONG AGO, a friend of mine who covers the police beat for a local newspaper noted that a citizen had been arrested and charged with "obstructing governmental administration."

"But what did this guy do?" asked my friend. "What's his offense?" At first the deputies, somewhat taken aback, refused to tell him. But my friend persisted. Finally it came out. There had been a brawl the previous evening at a local Legion post. The accused, it seemed, had not assaulted the deputies on their arrival, nor had he bad-mouthed them. But somewhere in the mêlée he had taken a kick at a police dog named Quint. Now, in the cold light of day, he stood charged with *obstructing governmental administration.* After the story came out the sheriff saw the silly side of the situation, and ordered the charge dropped. Tough news for Quint, with his aching ribs, but a small victory for freedom of the press, and the English language.

Today, such petty misuses of language are all around us. Instead of being used to communicate, the words are employed—particularly by bureaucrats, politicians, and other figures in authority—to obscure, distort, and manipulate the truth. If magazine editors are to be effective they must develop a sixth sense for detecting, and smoking out, this kind of double-talk. When the air fills with such grandiose fog-words as *facilitate, utilize, prioritize,* and *finalize* then they must sharpen their blue pencils and jab through the verbiage to tell the readers in plain English what has really happened.

Verbal pollution takes many forms. Oh yes, Johnnie can't read and Jenny can't write. And the media fill our ears and eyes with Adspeak. Free Gifts. Thick Sliced Bacon. Tastes Good Like a Cigaret Should. Car 4 Sale. All Nite Snax . . . But the worst source of corrosion, I submit, lies with those who've had all the benefits of education. Perhaps much of the blame for this can be laid at the door of the teachers themselves, who are world champions when it comes to making simple things sound complicated. No longer is a child lazy or a cheat. Today, in the argot of education authorities, she is *motivationally deficient* or *ethically disoriented*. Never say a family is poor. That might bruise their feelings or, much more likely, offend the school board's own sense of gentility. Instead, say they are *economically disadvantaged*. In this topsy-turvy lexicon bullies are *insensitive to their peers* and dumb students are *exceptional*.

To be sure, some euphemisms are harmless. We all have a tendency to wrap heartache in cotton wool. Instead of saying a friend is dying, we say he has a *terminal affliction*. Later, we do not say he is dead, but that he is *deceased* or that he has *passed away*. Fair enough. We are buffering ourselves against a problem for which there is no solution. But aspiring editors should note that many individuals tend to wrap their meaning in cotton wool not because their heart aches, but because their notion of the social proprieties is affronted, because they wish to inflate their sense of self-importance, or because they are trying to convince us (and perhaps themselves) that no problem exists and that everything will be okay. It is embarrassing for a woman to say that her spouse was fired from his job. How much easier for everyone (including the victim?) to say that his *employment was terminated*. Now that could happen to anyone. In this genteel terminology there are no more prisons, just *correctional facilities*. Cars don't run out of gas, they *experience fuel starvation*. People don't curse any more, they *use epithets*. No one is deaf or blind, they merely have a *learning disability*. And, of course, citizens don't kick police dogs; they *obstruct governmental administration*.

YOUNG JUVENILES

Some of these cotton-wool phrases are comical. But, such is the power of language, they can also be used to distort our sense of reality. When society calls a nuclear-tipped missile a *Peacekeeper* and speaks in conversational tones of *kill-ratios* and *mega-deaths* then we come perilously close to those Nazis who blandly dismissed the horrors of the Holocaust as "the final solution of the Jewish problem."

If a bad or dangerous situation is wrapped in enough sugar candy it cannot be clearly understood, and thus has no chance of being changed or resolved. When a nuclear plant runs amok, a good editor should not let her writers refer to the disaster as an *event,* or even as a near *melt-down,* as if those radioactive rods were no more lethal than a pat of butter. When the president of a major auto-manufacturing company says the safety record of one of his models has *statistical acceptability,* the editor should cut behind the fancy footwork to discover how many people have been killed, and how many more are likely to be killed and maimed in the future by that particular defect in design. And when the president of the United States tells the American people a bare-faced lie he should not, subsequently, be permitted to write it off as an *inoperative statement,* a *mistake,* or a *simple error of judgment.*

Of course, not all verbal pollution is malicious, or even intentional. Sometimes it is used to emphasize a point—as in the case of *free gift*—and sometimes it is used out of a lack of appreciation for the value of words—as in the case of the Boston mayor who inveighed against the depredations of *young juveniles.* The word *gift* is, of course, derived from the Anglo-Saxon word *gifan,* to give. And unfree gift, one for which the recipient must pay, is a contradiction. Knowledge of the linguistic origins of a word, or a class of words, can help an editor smoke out this kind of pollution. The city mayor could have saved himself a red face if he'd known that the word *juvenile* comes from the Latin *iuvenis,* young man.

Here are some other terminological redundancies that get by editors again and again. The house was *completely destroyed.* The composer *finally died* in 1910. The man was an *unprincipled lecher/wife beater/ murderer.* He had a *fertile imagination.* She was an *unfortunate victim.* Some redundancies are tougher to spot. *Creative artist? Cognitive thought?* A good test is to take the first word and replace it with one of opposite meaning; if the resulting phrase becomes a logical impossibility, then the use of the original word was unnecessary, and it should be eliminated. Is it possible to have an *un*creative artist? Or a *non*cognitive thought? Perhaps. An artist whose work is unoriginal and derivative might be called uncreative. Cognitive comes from the Latin *cognoscere,* to know. Unknowing thought, thought without knowledge as a kind of reverie or daydream is just possible. But we have probably stretched a point in both cases, and the author of the piece you are editing probably had no intention of conveying such a nuance to his readers. Here are some more redundant phrases. *Brief instant. Authentically true. Mentally insane. Personal friend. True facts. Legitimate rights. Stupid idiot. Unverified rumor. Newlywed bride . . .* You get the idea.

It is difficult, if not impossible, for an editor to combat verbal pollution and harness the submerged energies of the language if he or she has no understanding of its origins and how it evolved over the millennia. English is, primarily, a volatile amalgam of Latin, Old Norse, German, and Norman French. Major contributions have also been made by the Celts, the Arabs, and the Greeks. But the resulting fabric of words and grammar is far more powerful, and far more flexible, than the sum of all its varied parts. Today, the speaker of modern English can draw upon a total of some 500,000 words, or three times the total of modern German and five times that of modern French. The disparity in the number of words is doubled yet again when slang and new-minted technological terms are added to the verbal stew. But numerical superiority is the least of it. Behind the compilation of entries in English dictionaries lies a grammar that, by its internal logic, generally pushes the thoughts of its users into the path of clarity. At the same time, that grammar is also flexible enough to assimilate new terms and phrases that permit those thoughts to be expressed vividly and succinctly. One of English's particular strengths, when compared to other languages, is its ability to turn nouns into verbs, and verbs into nouns. We can board a *jet*, and then *jet* to Paris. We can *track* a satellite, and then plot its *track* on a chart. (Sometimes, however, things can go too far. On a recent flight the attendant wheeled up to us with a drinks cart. "Have you two been *beveraged* yet?" she asked.)

Such unusual capabilities have helped make English the language of international trade, diplomacy, communications, and popular culture. They have also had the unfortunate effect of causing it to infiltrate many of its competing languages. This phenomenon has, in recent years, produced such hybrids as Swinglish (Swedish English), Spanglish (Spanish English), Japlish (Japanese English), and Franglais (French English). The Académie Française has taken a dim view of such intrusions, but its efforts to police phrases like *jumbo jet* and *fast food* out of the language seem doomed to failure; a recent survey showed that one in every twenty words used by French people in day-to-day conversation is an anglicism.

The power of English stems, in large part, from the historical fact that Britain is an island lying near, but not too near, the coast of Europe. Successive waves of invaders swept across the Continent, often destroying the local inhabitants and eliminating their languages. Several moved on to invade Britain, but for logistical reasons were unable to exert the same dominance over the peoples of the island. Celts, Romans, Angles, Jutes, Saxons, Norse, and Normans came to Britain, but their conquests were partial and each was compelled to reach some compromise with the existing inhabitants, both in terms of territory and in terms of culture. Then, after the initial animosities subsided, the process of cross-fertilization would begin. If the newcomers did not have a name for a newly encountered vegetable or animal, then they would probably adopt the word used by the natives. And if the natives had no term for the strange tools and customs of the invader, they would probably return the linguistic compliment.

"In the common words we use every day," wrote Owen Barfield in his *History in English Words*, "the souls of past races, and the thoughts of individual men stand around us, not dead, but frozen in their attitudes like the courtiers in the garden of the sleeping beauty." If we understand the origin and the evolution of those words and savor the perception that went into their creation then, he says, that appreciation "circulates like blood through the whole of literature and life about us. It is the kiss which brings the sleeping courtiers to life."

Some sleeping courtiers — like the words *daughter*, *night* and *star* — have remained essentially unchanged for thousands of years. Examining their slow modification over the millennia can be likened to looking backwards down a telescope into the very beginnings of human consciousness. Take the word *daughter*. This is derived from the Anglo-Saxon *dohtor*, which came into the language when the peoples of Friesland and southern Denmark voyaged across the North Sea in the fifth century. *Dohtor* can, in turn, be traced back to the old Indo-European *dhugheter*, meaning the sucker of milk from a teat or *dug*.

Most occidental languages trace their roots back to Indo-European, the tongue spoken by the Aryans; these people dwelt, some twenty thousand years ago, along the banks of the Dnieper river. For an unknown reason — perhaps it was overpopulation or a radical change in climate — the Aryans began, two thousand years before the birth of Christ — to expand outward from their homelands. One movement swept east and south around the shores of the Black Sea into Persia and then over the mountains into India. Along the way *dhugheter* became the Persian *duhitar* and the Sanskrit *duhita*. Another great segment of Aryans thrust westward, and then fanned out in a series of waves that produced the Anglo-Saxon *dohtor*, the Greek *thygeter* in the south, and after a trek of several thousand miles across Scandinavia and half the North Atlantic ocean, the Icelandic word *dottir*.

THE LAND OF THE EVENING

The gradual evolution of the old Aryan words tells us, like a sleeping beauty brought to life, something about the conditions encountered on that extraordinary exodus. The very word *Europe* stems from the ancient Indo-European word *ereb*, meaning shadow or evening. When viewed from the banks of the Dnieper in south Russia, the mysterious country to the west, whose trackless forests were only illuminated as the sun went down at the end of the day, came to be known as *Erepe*, or Europe, the Land of the Evening.

The tribes that swept westward across Northern Europe encountered animals and plants that were unfamiliar to them. To name the new phenomena such beautiful words as *beech, elm,* and *hazel* came into the language. The birds of the new temperate climate were named *finch, starling,* and *swallow.* These words are common to most European languages, but they are unknown in Sanskrit, so philologists have concluded that the encounter with beech trees and swallows came after the Aryan peoples divided into their two great expansive movements.

One of the earliest waves of Aryan peoples moved southward into what is now Greece. They founded several important cities and minted whole families of new words to describe their evolving thoughts and feelings. *Academy, philosophy, poetry, grammar, rhythm, logic, melody* — all came into the language at this time. On the darker side, the Attic Greeks also found it necessary to describe certain political conditions with words like *tyrant* and *despot* (derived from the Aryan *poti-s,* meaning lord, husband, powerful). Their linguistic contributions contrasted sharply with those of another tribe that had moved over the top of Greece into Italy. Such words as *authority, command, dictator, dominion, rule,* and *officer* now entered the language and the neo-Romans began their long climb to the creation of their *empire.* Greeks and Romans were both familiar with government by a single individual, yet the words *dictator* and *tyrant* evoke a wholly different response in those who hear them. A dictator can be sane, businesslike, even benign. But a tyrant is a madman, with drool on his lips and blood on his hands. The language we use inevitably colors our perception of reality. Could it be that the contrasting views of power gave the Greeks their *democracy* and the Romans their world *dominion*?

It is interesting to speculate how two peoples, originally joined in both race and language, could turn out so differently. Perhaps their contrast in culture can be attributed to geographical differences. But both peoples moved into warm, sunlit peninsulas of comparable size and terrain. The chief dissimilarity is that Greece, unlike Italy, is washed by seas strung with several necklaces of island *archipelagos* (from the Greek *pelagos,* sea, which in turn stems from the ancient Aryan *pla-k,* meaning wide, or flat.) Is it pure chance that democracy began in Athens? A glance at a map of the Peloponnesian Wars shows the Athenian League to be composed of all the islands in the Aegean and all the coastal communities bordering on that sea, while its opponents, led by Sparta, were primarily inland states.

Island dwellers have a distinctive frame of mind. It is relatively easy for them to protect themselves against intruders. Hostile ships can be spotted while they are still many miles away. The islanders can tackle them at the vulnerable moment of disembarkation. Or, if the enemy is of overwhelming strength, they have time to clamber into their own boats and escape over the horizon. This defensive moat of water builds a sense of security and encourages those who dwell on islands to settle their disputes without recourse to outside adventurists. One man may disagree, even quarrel, with another man without attempting to slaughter him or expecting to be slaughtered by him. And that, after all, would seem to be the essence of democracy. Is it chance that the two oldest modern democracies — Iceland and Britain — were both nurtured upon island terrain? Why is it that such open forms of government did not flourish in continental Europe? Or in Asia?

BOGS AND BANSHEES

From about 1,000 B.C. onwards waves of Celts began to move across the North Sea into Britain and brought with them some beautiful words including *avon* (water), *glen, bard, bog,* and *banshee.* But they were driven by successive waves of Romans, Jutes, Angles, and Saxons into the hills of Wales and Scotland and across the sea to Ireland. The Romans, making their first successful invasion shortly after the birth of Christ, spread a series of camps, or *castra,* across the countryside; these came to form the last syllables of such place names as Winchester, Lancaster, and Gloucester. The Romans also gave us the names of our months. Most are simply named, in stalwart military fashion, after numbers or former emperors (*July* and *August*). But *January* is named after Janus, the godlike creature who guarded the gate of heaven and could look backwards and forwards, into the old year and into the new. *April,* the month when buds, limbs, and hearts unfold, is derived from the Latin *aperire,* to open.

The days of the week, except for Saturday, come from the Norse and the Teutons. The word *day* itself is taken from the Aryan concept of *dawn* or simply an open sky. Sunday is named after the Norse god Sunna. Moon-day. Tues-day is derived from a Teutonic version of Zeus. Wednesday is for Woden, Thursday for his son Thor, and Friday is for his lady Fricka.

A picture of the Teutons' long trek through the densely wooded terrain of northern Europe is to be had from the word *weary*, derived from a verb meaning to tramp over wet ground. Human settlements were few and separated by dark dripping forests in which lurked *wolves, bear* (from *bera*, the brown one), *elves, goblins*, and *trolls*. Small wonder then that an age without firearms, cold steel, or Christian faith came to derive the word *fear* from *fare*, a journey, or the feeling one might expect upon a journey. Before a traveler set out into the mists he would check his route out with a *learned* village elder, for *learn* traces back to a word meaning "follow a track." In any such journey, the presence of a domesticated dog, or *hound* would give warning of danger ahead, and would have helped greatly in any struggle with wild beasts. The Aryan word for dog was *kun*, which became *hund* in Anglo-Saxon, *canis* in Latin, and *kyon* in Greek. Later, this Greek word became a nickname for a school of philosophy, the *Cynics*, because they believed in nothing and snarled at every new idea like dogs. Because of the large number of wild dogs infesting a group of islands off the Atlantic coast of Africa, Columbus named them Islas Canarias, and this is how a beautiful bird, also a resident of those islands, came to be known as a *canary*.

The ancient Aryan word for womb was *guelbh*, which inspired the Greek *delphys* (cub or calf from the womb). Also derived from this root are the words *Dauphin* (the cub of the French king) and *dolphin*, the fish that does not lay eggs but has cubs from a womb.

As the Angles and the Saxons moved into eastern England, they scooped up two new collections of words, probably from their neighbors to the south. The first group suggests that the tough hunters and fishermen were coming in out of the cold and savoring some of the finer things in life. The words *kettle, dish, pillow, kitchen, mill, street*, and *table* now enter the language, closely followed by an even more elevating group of words: *altar, hymn, psalm, martyr, priest*, and *nun*. But the new faith was not much help in fighting off the new devil, manifested in the form of Viking longships. These men, descended from the Norse branch of the Aryan family, sacked and burned their way through the new coastal enclaves. Later, they too came to settle in the fair green land and brought with them such words as *hit, knife, take*, and the more complex words *wrong, law, outlaw, hustings*, and *moot*. The word *wrong* is particularly interesting. It comes from *wringen* to compress, strain, or twist. The normal code of behavior had been twisted, and retribution under *law* was appropriate. Perhaps, in a way, the Norse were fairer than their victims. Presumably the word *wrong* entered the language at this point because there was no clear concept of it in Anglo-Saxon thought. It may be hard to conceive of a community so barbarous as to have, beyond tribal fealty, no notion of right and wrong. And yet, today we have our muggers and our mafiosi who clearly believe that anything becomes theirs if they can muster the strength to take it.

The word *barbarous* traces back to the Aryan *baba*, meaning to babble or stammer (which is what *babies* and *barbarians* do). The Aryan word for home or camp is *kei*. This in turn inspired the Anglo-Saxon *ham*, from which is derived *hamlet* and *home*. It was the home or the flames of the camp hearth to which the *ghosts* (from the Indo-European *ghostis*, meaning foreigner or *guest*) or dead spirits were drawn. While treated with awe, these apparitions were not necessarily a source of terror to the pre-Christian mind; *ghosts* could, in fact, be welcomed as *guests*. Pagan ceremony required that large fires be lit deep in the forest to guide lost spirits home and to assure them they had not been forgotten. Christian missionaries frowned on such practices but they could not stop them, so, making light of a bad job, they crowned the ancient rituals with the purgative All Saints' Day, also known as All Hallows' Day; now the spooks come out of the night to be propitiated and blessed on Hallows' eve, or *Halloween*.

THE NEW GENTILITY

William the Conquerer made the last successful invasion of England in 1066, and brought with him a host of words bespeaking a new military technology: *fortress, lance, banner, assault, battle*. But the Normans did not exterminate the resident Anglo-Saxons. Instead, while letting them keep their contemptible common law, they reduced them to a state of bondage. The decline of the Saxon race under the Norman yoke can be traced in the transformation of the word *ceorl*, a leader with substantial military authority (as in *earl*) to the word *churl*, a serflike creature who slept with the pigs in return for a little seed corn each spring.

Other Norman words hint at their preoccupation with gentility. These are *master, servant, butler, parlor*, and *banquet*. But they also imported some useful concepts for the administration of the new subject race. *Burglar, felon, judge, court*, all came into the language, along with *contract, heir* (and hence *hierarchy*), *jury, lease*, and *mortgage*. The contrast between the Anglo-Saxon and Norman words for domestic animals is intriguing. Here are some examples:

Anglo-Saxon	Norman
oxen	beef
sheep	mutton
calves	veal
swine	pork

A sharp social distinction underlies these two lists, and it has lent an invidious warp to the language ever since. While the Saxons were outdoors under the sun and moon, herding and caring for these animals as living creatures, the Norman gentry were up in the castle enjoying them as varieties of food steaming upon a wooden trencher. One result of this split is that Anglo-Saxon words tend to be sensual, vivid, and direct while Norman French — and thus Latin — tends to produce words that are genteel, lifeless, and abstract. Much of today's jargon and verbal pollution, I suspect, stems from Norman England.

Every language has an interior logic of its own and a structure of implied values that in large part determines the speaker's view of society and the mode in which he thinks. The division between Saxon and Norman England reflects, in a different setting, the ancient cultural split between Greece and Rome, between the desire for freedom and the drive for order, between democracy and dominion. Those overeducated persons who nowadays pollute the air with pretentious abstractions are, in many ways, reincarnations of the eleventh-century Normans. They use the language; and with the vocabulary come the self-importance and the polarizing attitudes. Why employ the Latinate *intersection* when one can easily use the bold and picturesque *crossroads*? Why say *facilitate* and *terminate* when one can say *help* and *end*? The Saxons were seeing and feeling while the Normans were cerebrating and devising new embellishments for their administrative regulations. For these reasons the magazine editor should eschew Norman English. He or she is likely to achieve far more impact from a head or a lead composed of short, vivid words of Anglo-Saxon origin.

It has been rightly said by the authors of *The Story of English* that the genius of our colloquial day-to-day language is essentially egalitarian and democratic. "It has given expression to the voice of freedom from Wat Tyler, to Tom Paine, to Thomas Jefferson, to Edmund Burke, to the Chartists, to Abraham Lincoln, to the Suffragettes, to Winston Churchill, to Martin Luther King."

Churchill, as much as any of these individuals, was aware that jargon and circumlocution can be used to confuse, obscure, and cover up the truth. As one of the leading statesmen of his era, he knew that such heavy-handed usages of language are generally authoritarian in both intention and effect. And, as a writer and journalist of renown, he also knew that the expression of ideas in clear, straightforward prose can exert an enormous leverage in the struggle to preserve individual freedom. In 1940, when an ill-prepared Britain stood alone against the armed might of the Third Reich, Churchill exhorted his people to resist the anticipated Nazi invasion with this simple — indeed, almost rudimentary — series of images: "We shall fight on the beaches, we shall fight on the landing grounds, we shall fight in the fields and in the streets, we shall fight in the hills; we shall never surrender." It is interesting to note that all but one of the words in this evocative sentence are derived from Anglo-Saxon; only the contemptible *surrender* is of Norman origin.

The point, I'm sure, will not be lost on aspiring magazine editors and writers. The growing host of bureaucrats, facilitators, and other neo-Norman obscurantists may strive to make themselves more secure, and more important, by hiding behind a linguistic barricade of *terminations, intersections,* and *utilizations.* But it is the duty of all journalists, as the spiritual descendants of the ancient Saxons, to be neither awed nor hoodwinked by such pretentious verbiage. They must acquire a special taste for puncturing managerial pomposity. And they must learn how to cut through all the obfuscation and put matters into plain English so that everyone can understand what is happening, and what is not happening.

For further reading see:
Owen Barfield, *History in English Words;* Mario Pei, *The Families of Words;* J. C. Hixon and I. Colodny, *Word Ways;* Albert C. Baugh, *History of the English Language;* C. S. Lewis, *Studies in Words;* Mary Dohan, *Our Own Words;* and Robert McCrum, William Cran, and Robert MacNeil, *The Story of English.*

12

MAGAZINE MANAGEMENT
Starting Your Own Magazine

ONE NIGHT LATE IN APRIL 1976, James and Elinor Campbell Lawrence stepped back from the kitchen table of the farmhouse they had rented in Ontario, Canada, and reviewed their handiwork. Ever since they had been students together at an American university they had dreamed of designing, editing, and producing a magazine of their own. Now their dream was turning into reality. Before them on the table, glistening amid the piles of clipped photos, gluepots, and discarded coffee mugs, sat the dummy issue of *Harrowsmith*. Named after the nearby village, the new magazine was aimed at an audience of do-it-yourselfers interested in growing their own food and designing, building, and furnishing their own homes. The first issue ran 64 pages in length and featured an immense tomato colored a most unpalatable hue of green. A smudge of lipstick lay on the tomato's flank, and the cover blurb ran: "Kissing Supermarkets Good-by." Within weeks, a printer had produced 25,000 copies of *Harrowsmith*, and 15,000 of these were mailed, with an invitation to subscribe, to most of the Canadian readers of an American magazine called *Organic Gardening*.

"We just couldn't believe the response," says Elinor. "Some people said we'd be okay if we got 6 percent, while others said 4 percent would be fine. In fact, we got a favorable response from more than 20 percent of the recipients." Elinor and James, then aged twenty-six and twenty-nine respectively, used the new subscription money to pay the printer for their issue and get the second issue under way. Soon they were hiring several villagers part-time to help them with paperwork and subscription lists. The Lawrences were permitted to use an abandoned bank building as their office, rent-free, on condition that they kept the place in good repair.

By 1980 *Harrowsmith* and its affiliated enterprises employed some thirty-six people and its offices had moved to an old nineteen-room mansion across the road. Circulation went up steadily so that it topped 160,000 by the spring of 1981, yielding total revenues of more than $4 million a year. The magazine has also received more than thirty awards for writing, photography, and graphic design, and has opened its own bookstore in the old bank building, featuring volumes on everything from energy saving to child rearing. In the late 1970s *Harrowsmith* hired the computer services of one of Canada's major magazine distribution houses, but things got so fouled up that Lawrence went to a group of computer science graduates at Queen's University and had them design a special program to handle *Harrowsmith's* subscription sales and renewals. This program became the model for many other magazines in both Canada and the United States.

THE DREAM

Most people have a dream. Perhaps you dream of starring in a smash-hit Broadway musical. Or it's your fancy to quarterback a team to victory in the Super Bowl. For my part I have always been intrigued by the idea of operating a gambling casino like Rick's place in the movie *Casablanca*. Each person's dream is necessarily unique to him or her. Yet a surprisingly common ambition is to start a magazine of one's own. James Kobak, an accountant who has become a well-known broker of magazine properties, is familiar with the potency of this particular dream. "I have the impression," he says, "that every man, woman, and child in the United States has an idea for the one magazine that is 'needed' by the American public." For many citizens, however, the dream of starting a magazine explodes with the first realistic survey of what is required of any would-be publisher. But even then some 300 intrepid souls each year attempt to make this ultimate dream come true.

"The chances of making it are brutally grim," one investment banker told a *New York Times* reporter not long ago. Even an experienced publisher with substantial capital and elaborate polling services cannot place the odds of success at better than one in two. And the odds of an aspiring publisher without capital or executive experience surviving the first two years are one in ten.

THREE WAYS TO GO

The Lawrences beat the odds. Was it luck? Or did they possess special insights that let them sidestep the usual bear traps strewn across the paths of aspiring publishers? This chapter cannot assure success for you if you are intent upon trying to start a new magazine. But it may help you avoid some of the more obvious mistakes and thereby diminish the chances of your becoming one more publishing statistic. Basically, there are three ways of establishing a new magazine. They might be called

1. The Big Store Caper
2. Subchapter S
3. The Church Mouse Squeak

The Lawrences' *Harrowsmith* is an example of the Church Mouse Squeak. They were as poor as church mice when they began, yet they somehow managed to squeak through every crisis. The only way they could raise funds for their initial mailing was to pledge the family station wagon as collateral for a $3,500 loan. Then each new advance or expansion — and this is an important Church Mouse principle — was carefully attuned to the resources available.

The so-called Subchapter S approach basically requires the founding publisher to obtain financing by surrendering some control of his publication to partners or investors. Some notable examples of this mode have been *Equus*, the highly successful horse magazine, and *National Lampoon*, published by Leonard Mogel. But in an important sense the investment approach comes to resemble the Church Mouse Squeak; if you can't persuade conventional sources of financing like an investment bank to lend you money, then you may have trouble sandbagging a private investor to make any sizable contribution to your cause.

In contrast to these two, we have the Big Store Caper. Conde Nast's *Self*, a self-improvement magazine aimed at young working women, spent eighteen months and $20 million in planning and preparation before the first issues appeared in January 1979. Nearly a decade later Frances Lear, the former wife of TV producer Norman Lear, spent two years and an estimated $15 million to bring *Lear's*, for sophisticated over-40s women, into existence. The Big Store approach has not always produced success, even in the hands of established publishing houses. True, *Penthouse* begat the successful and futuristic *Omni*. And the National Geographic Society has produced its *Traveller*. But Time Inc. pumped millions into the science magazine *Discover* before selling it off, and spent an estimated $100 mil-

Fig. 24. *Harrowsmith* enterprises filled this nineteen-room mansion just five years after this station wagon was pledged as collateral for a $3,500 bank loan. Courtesy *Harrowsmith*.

lion on *TV Cable Week*, only to kill it off after the third issue. Such magazines as *Geo, Families* (put out by *Reader's Digest*), and *US* (the New York *Times*'s imitation of *People*) have undoubtedly brought their parents more grief than joy. For this reason, declares James Kobak, "publishing companies rarely are the founders of major new magazines." For the most part "they let others take the initial risk and buy them out when profits have been assured."

THE SEAWEED FACTOR

Why is starting a new magazine so chancy?

The short answer to this question is: All the research polls and audience surveys before publication are, in effect, trying to measure the unmeasurable and to quantify ideas and feelings that are, by their very nature, imponderable. There is a strange phenomenon — call it the Seaweed Factor — that brings home to perfection the problems confronting the

Fig. 25. James Lawrence tells the author and members of seminar in magazine management at Syracuse University how he started *Harrowsmith* and about his plans for launching a new magazine called *Equinox*. In 1986 he established an editorially distinct American version of *Harrowsmith*.

new publisher. When a descriptive brochure of a magazine is mailed to prospective readers, it generally stimulates a far heavier response than a similar mailing that includes a sample copy of the projected publication.

This is the Seaweed Factor. It is derived from the old horror movies. Good directors know that it is far more terrifying for an audience to be denied a glimpse of the Monster from the Deep. The hissing breath, the silently turning doorknob, the seaweed strewn along the corridor — all these evoke a deeper apprehension than the sight of any fanged, plastic-coated troll conceived by Hollywood. In the same way, a brochure evokes a stronger response than the sample magazine because human nature tends to judge the potential more fascinating than the actual. For this reason pollsters and demographic researchers operate upon ground more slippery than the floor of any monster's cave.

A new magazine, to be successful, must meet three basic requirements:

    1. It must have an idea or concept that appeals to a group of people (or readership) in a way that no other publication or medium can.

Fig. 26. Bringing the three components into productive alignment: some new magazine starts.

2. It must have a readership large enough — generally at least 100,000 — to sustain financial equilibrium.

3. It must have a readership whose purchasing power appeals to advertisers.

On any healthy, mature publication these three elements are inextricably entwined. But even if the new publisher is going the Big Store route, the idea must precede the readership, which in turn must precede the mustering of advertisers. True, it is possible — in the back-assed way employed by some politicians — for an entrepreneur to bustle out and poll people about what kind of magazine they'd like, and then retire to the drawing board and design a publication that fits the bill. But in the great majority of cases the would-be publisher gets the idea, acquires a readership, and then presents them on a plate to the advertisers. Even for a publication that bears all the marks of success, this takes time, perhaps as much as four or five years. Thus a fourth factor joins the other three:

4. Sufficient capital to sustain the operation while its three primary components are falling into productive alignment.

Established Big Store publishers dance onto the stage full-blown. They have honed their editorial concept, acquired a sizable readership with pilot copy sales, and have used their advertising contacts to drum up a fairly solid selection of ads in their opening issues. Whether this rather synthetic plant takes root and produces its own fruit is an open question. If it does, the publisher may have another *Sports Illustrated*, which cost Time Inc. some $30 million before it began to make money. If the plant doesn't take root it may leave its sponsors millions in the hole, as in the case of Gruner and Jahr's *Geo* and McCall's *Your Place*, a brave attempt to imitate the highly successful *Apartment Life*, now renamed *Metropolitan Home*.

SUBCHAPTER S

Most readers of this book, however, do not have $20 million or even $1 million to spare for a Big Store Caper, so I shall assume that if you are to start your own magazine it will be by some other means. A major advocate of the Subchapter S approach (and its less frequently used cousins, the Partnership and the Section 1244 investment corporation) is the courtly magazine broker James Kobak. The precise structure of the Subchapter S (its poetic name is derived from a legislative regulation) varies from publication to publication, but it basically requires a group of fewer than ten investors to buy a single class of stock in the new venture.

If the project fails, the subscribers write it off as a tax loss. If it succeeds they stand to make a very substantial profit. This approach is necessarily more formal, and legalistic, and ultimately quite a bit more expensive than that of the Church Mouse Squeak. Jim Kobak has written extensively of his strategies in a series of articles in *Folio*, the Magazine for Magazine Managements (published at 911 Hope Street, Stamford, Conn. 06907). Kobak advises would-be publishers to take a two-tier approach to financing their new magazines. Primary financing requires the raising of between $70,000 and $100,000. Most of this is used to conduct an extensive survey of potential readers. If the idea goes over well — that is, in Kobak's terms, if there is a positive response from at least 4 percent of those polled — then that initial investment group tries to attract between $500,000 and $2 million in venture capital. This secondary financing requires a further sacrifice of control by the new publisher, but it enables him or her to hire experienced staff and establish offices and so forth up front, long before the first issue of the magazine appears.

This is a kind of poor man's version of the Big Store Caper. It seeks to employ other people's money in a series of gradually escalating steps. If the project's vital body signs begin to fade away at any time in the preparatory period, then it can be abandoned with a minimum of loss to all concerned. But the going is never easy. Jim Kobak says that as a new publisher, you must have "the persistence and strength to be turned down often, reach the brink of disaster a few times, and carry on anyway." At the same time you, the heroic individual attempting to make your big dream come true, must have "the strength of character to drop the project if you find that the world is not waiting for your magazine after all."

The first step, says Kobak, is to develop a business plan comprising fewer than twenty pages and organized under eight self-explanatory headings:

1. The concept stating the idea underlying your project
2. The editorial need
3. The markets, stressing the appeal of your audience to advertisers
4. The advertisers
5. The company, concerned with the details of organization and of primary and secondary financing
6. The competition
7. The people involved, staff members, their qualifications
8. Financial projections, through first four years' operation

SEED MONEY

Kobak estimates that the major component of the $75,000 primary or seed money after legal fees is likely to be spent on the devising and execution of a direct-mail test to some 100,000 potential subscribers. The creation, the angling, and the timing of such tests have become a minor art form, and Kobak suggests that it be handed over to professionals. Their final report, if it is favorable, is likely to be of substantial help to you in your efforts to acquire secondary financing from hard-eyed venture capitalists.

The chief problem of the Subchapter S approach is that even under the most favorable conditions the publisher's share of the project dwindles very fast. Say you need $75,000 and sell 75 percent of your Subchapter S stock to ten investors, each of whom puts up $7,500. Your own contribution is your idea and your willingness to work and worry sixteen hours a day to make it a reality. For this you get 25 percent — nominally worth $25,000 — of the original stock. The idea tests out and you go for secondary financing. The merchant banks like it enough to put up $1.5 million, but they want 60 percent of the action in return. The overall picture is shown in figure 27. Your original investment has now risen ten times

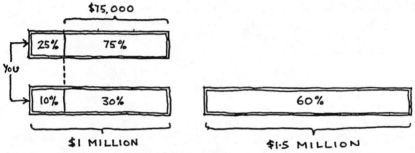

Fig. 27. Financing with Subchapter S, 1.

in nominal value, from $25,000 to $250,000. But you only control 10 percent of total stock. If your original partners or your secondary investors want to change or make over your editorial concept, it is easy for them to do so. Indeed, they can vote you out of a job with the twirl of a phone dial. If you are to retain some clout in the final lineup — say 30 percent — then it means you must retain some 75 percent of the stock in the Subchapter S corporation. The whole picture as it now looks is shown in figure 28.

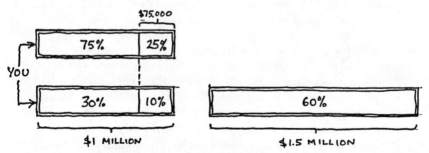

Fig. 28. Financing with Subchapter S, 2.

When the secondary financing is completed you hold title to stock nominally worth $750,000. This is nice for you, but the notion of your Subchapter S investors letting you retain such a massive chunk of the action — when your only contribution has been a bright but untried idea — is absurd. In short, if you retain anything like 75 percent of Subchapter S stock you are unlikely to get even a nibble of interest from a primary investor. If your silver tongue can con them into such a deal, you are eloquent enough to arrange your financing elsewhere. It is at this point that the Subchapter S approach collapses into the Church Mouse Squeak. And the latter has the advantage of leaving you, when all the fancy footwork is over, in charge of the store.

THE CHURCH MOUSE SQUEAK

This scenario, employed so effectively by the Lawrences, gets much of its energy from challenging the conventional modes of starting a magazine. Commenting upon what he terms "the established dicta and dogmas of publishing," James Lawrence notes with a Churchillian glint in his eye that "occasionally we didn't believe in them, often we couldn't afford them and, not infrequently, we had never heard of them." Bascially, the Church Mouse Squeak requires that you conceive of an idea that has enough traction to pull you through the difficulties into the hearts of a readership capable of sustaining the publication by subscription, without benefit of very much advertising.

Most advertisers do not want to associate their client's product with a losing venture. When they grasp that the new publication is freestanding and doesn't really need them — and this may take them two or three years — then they are likely to crowd in for a piece of the action. For advertisers, nothing succeeds like success. When they finally come calling, many a struggling publisher has been tempted to invite them to take that long, refreshing plunge onto the sidewalks of Madison Avenue. But generally he bites his tongue and takes the order.

THE IDEA

For a Church Mouse, a powerful idea is the most important thing of all. You don't have the big bucks to hype it, to stuff it into the minds of potential readers. The idea has to be good enough to promote itself. Bernard Goldhirsh had a good idea. He graduated from MIT in 1961 and went to work as an engineer for Northrop Aviation and Polaroid. But he had been bitten by the sailing bug and, for a few extra dollars, began moonlighting as an instructor in celestial navigation. His students, however, wanted to know more about sailing than navigation. The established magazine in the field, *Yachting*, seemed to assume that everyone knew all the ropes. Why not, he wondered, start a magazine full of how-to articles for sailing novices? In January 1970 the thirty-year-old Goldhirsh borrowed $20,000 from friends and put out his first issue of *Sail*. Five years later *Sail* topped *Yachting* in circulation, and Goldhirsh was on his way to establishing several new ventures, including the highly successful *Inc.* designed to be read by small-business owners who felt themselves ignored by such giants as *Business Week* and *Fortune*. A good idea has traction. It moves forward on its own.

SOCIAL TRENDS

Generally, if an idea is to be effective it must play into a major social trend. *Sail* magazine moved in on the fact that a new wave of affluent young professional people were becoming intrigued by the ancient sport of sailing. If a new magazine is to ride such a trend and successfully encroach upon an established competitor, then it must educate its readers as it goes along. How-to articles are the staple of trend-riders. The infant *New York* magazine encroached upon the *New Yorker's* sacred turf by eschewing literary *pensées* for hard-nosed items such as how to organize a rent strike. In the same way *Country Journal* rode the how-tos of rural living deep into *Yankee's* established territory. Service pieces appeal to newcomers, active hands-on people who are likely to go out and buy the tools and toys they need to exercise their new knowledge. The readers of Goldhirsh's *Sail*, as their know-how deepened, were ready to make ever more expensive purchases of boats and gear, to the joy of a growing circle of advertisers.

How does one spot an emerging social trend?

An examination of population statistics and demographics can be both helpful and misleading. Just because a large number of people are associated with a topic doesn't mean they want to read about it. "There are 40 million washing machines in the U.S.," observes Joe Hansen, the publisher of *Folio* magazine, "but I doubt anyone would buy a magazine about washing machines."

A better approach, perhaps, is to check out your own interests and note how they changed over the last few years. The lifestyles of your neighbors are also worthy of examination. Is everyone engaged in some new activity? Fly fishing? Wind surfing? Indoor tennis? Bridge parties? Cross-country skiing? Art tours? Are people wanting to find out about such topics and are other people waiting to sell them the necessary equipment?

Sometimes eager manufacturers can supply equipment when none is necessary. The jogging craze has passed its peak, but for years it represented a triumph of merchandising. It transformed *Runner's World* from a newsletter to a plush four-color monthly. Hundreds of millions of dollars worth of suits and track shoes were sold to people who really only needed a T-shirt, shorts, and scuffed-up sneakers to get in motion.

THE PROSUMER

An aspiring publisher would do well to check out the work of sociologists. Alvin Toffler's *Third Wave* gives some intriguing pointers. Our average citizen, because of improved medical care and lower birth rates, is getting older. There are fewer families and they are, apparently, becoming less child-centered. Toffler singles out two other major agents of coming social change. The revolution in electronics, he believes, will "demassify" our communications and enable society to function effectively in smaller groups. Large corporations have been leaving the major cities for more than a decade now. Electronic hookups will make it possible for brainworkers to transact their business in smaller plants, or even at home. This decentralizing is further enhanced by the rising cost of energy. Why travel, when you can plug in electronically? And why plug into the power company when you can go into the back yard and fell some winter fuel?

Are the great metropolises doomed, crime-ridden, energy-consuming husks? Or will there be an urban renaissance premised on tougher immigration laws and more equitable taxation? Will the possession of leisure time and timeflex (the ability to perform work at times convenient to you) become more important than the possession of things? Will what you do become more important than what you own? Toffler predicts that the next decades will see the rise of the "prosumer," who is defined as someone who consumes what he has produced. If you grow your own vegetables, fix your own plumbing, or insulate your own house you are a prosumer. He cites a revealing statistic. In 1975 individuals for the first time bought more hand tools than the construction industry. The trend to "prosumption" is likely to increase as the work of "professional" plumbers and carpenters and their like becomes more expensive. Why stand by and watch a mason patch up your back-yard patio when you know, by consulting your latest issue of *Household Handiman*, that you can do a better job and save the hourly wage (plus state tax)? The difference will bring you several dinners for two. Indeed, why eat micro-ovened goodies in a restaurant when you can, with the aid of *Cuisine*, presume a *cordon bleu* repast in your own home?

The concept of prosumption is likely to take deeper and deeper hold of society if the services of government and professional trades people decline in quality. Not only is it cheaper; the prosumer also has the profound satisfaction of achieving something with his or her own hands. There may be a few jagged edges to the homemade patio but, by God, we hauled the stone and laid it out ourselves. Such handwork offers profound satisfactions in a society increasingly dominated by headwork occupations. In general, the trend to prosumption is so profound, and so multifarious in its dimensions that a thousand aspiring editors could play into it without treading on one another's toes.

THE DUMMY

Let us say you identify an appealing trend in the desire of an increasing number of people to finish, restore, and even construct from scratch their own house furniture. You consult the *U.S. Statistical Abstract* and *U.S. Chamber of Commerce* surveys and discover that last year 2.2 million Americans spent $800 million on unfinished furniture, up 200 percent on the amount spent ten years ago. The number of stores selling sanders and other finishing tools has tripled in the last decade. Two books on the subject have had excellent sales. One magazine called *Masterpiece* dominates the market. But it disdains how-tos for plushly illustrated pieces on antique furniture collections. You've had some experience editing the sales brochures of the Johnson Tool Co.; and after much discussion with your friends, you decide to explore the possibilities of starting a new bimonthly magazine that you will call *Veneer*.

You hope you can persuade the Johnson Tool Co. to give or sell you the names and addresses of the 150,000 do-it-yourselfers who receive the free brochure each year. But before you make your pitch to them it is necessary to develop a twenty-page business plan of your magazine and, if possible, produce a "dummy," or sample first copy. When outlining your proposal, avoid vague generalities. Kobak cites a typical example of up-beat vacuity. "The magazine will be bright, witty, and chatty — serious without being ponderous. We will take a stand, but not go out of our way to be controversial." All this sounds good but, as Kobak points out, what does it really say? Not much. The only way to pin down a new magazine concept, he says, is to compile a table of contents for at least the first six and preferably the first twelve issues of the publication. The title of each article should be followed by a brief summary of what the article is about, and how it attempts to interest or serve the reader.

An effective dummy requires that all the articles in the first issue be written out in full, printed up, and laid out with heads, decks, and art-work. To make your dummy even more realistic you might paste in typi-cal samples of full-page ads from Johnson and other manufacturers likely to be interested in your readership. Printing costs can be high. The Law-rences paid $800 in 1976 to have the *Harrowsmith* dummy set in type. Perhaps you can jawbone the printer of the tool-company brochure to do it on the cheap.

When you have laid out and pasted up the dummy, you can now make a pitch to Johnson Tool for the use of its list. More jawboning. If the company won't give it free, then perhaps you can tempt it with the offer of a free full-page ad in the first issue, 50 percent charges in the sec-ond, and full rates from then on.

It is now that the Church Mouse faces his or her first big expense. Flyers inviting the 150,000 readers of Johnson Tool's brochure must be writ-ten, printed up, and — most expensive of all — stuffed and mailed. If you have a pleasing mien perhaps you can persuade the printer to do it free, or to defer his bill until your subscriptions come in. Such things happen. A printer was so excited by the idea underlying the Lawrences' *Harrow-smith* that he agreed to defer the bill until the printing of the second issue.

Your mailing to Johnson's 150,000 list members will cost you about $45,000 at 30 cents a name. If you get a response significantly be-low 10 percent, then your idea in its present form lacks traction and, as a shrewd Church Mouse, you must either change it or quit. However, it should also be noted that even a high response rate is not conclusive; would-be publishers may be shocked to find that a third or more of those pledged subscribers default after seeing the first issue of the magazine. If you were not a Church Mouse and had substantial financial backing, then perhaps you could accept a far lower response rate. But the orange light is flashing.

THE CHASM

Let's say you get a favorable response from 15 percent of Johnson's brochure readers. Of these, say about one-third renege, and 13,000 readers send you the $15 subscription for six issues, or a year's worth of *Veneer*. At first you seem to be in clover, with $195,000 cash in hand. You march off to the printers and have 19,000 copies of the first issue produced. This costs you $15,200 and a further $3,900 when you mail out 13,000 to subscribers. You mail out 1,000 copies to influential people in the field and place the remaining 5,000 copies in strategic locations — by the cash registers of lumber, paint, and unfinished furniture stores — and with newsstand distribution agencies. Though distributing the newsstand copies is expensive, you tell yourself the exposure is good. You sell 1,600.

The details of income and expenditure for this pilot issue of *Veneer* are laid out in the first two columns of table 3. Besides the $19,100 devoted to printing and mailing, the issue has also cost you $25,000 in salaries, $6,000 in payments for free-lance editorial and artwork, and some $4,000 in rent and phone service. In short, you are paying out $54,100 to generate no more than $6,249 in newsstand sales and ad revenues. If circulation and the number of ads sold remain constant then you will probably go broke putting out issue no. 4 of *Veneer*. Eight out of ten new magazines generally plunge into the Chasm sometime during their first year, seldom to be heard of again. The basic problem, of course, is lack of working capital to boost the magazine on to a higher plateau of circulation where advertising and editorial matter will have a chance to come into productive alignment. A Big Store operation can keep barging along by just dipping into capital, but Church Mice often utter their last squeak as obligations swamp resources.

One way the resourceful Church Mouse can postpone his or her plunge into the Chasm is to slow down the publication's metabolism and — as we had *Veneer* do — produce not twelve but six issues a year. The elongated schedule permits more time for ad promotion, the solicitation of new readers, and the preparation of top-flight editorial copy. Sometimes a printer who would stick it to a Big Store operation with no qualms can be persuaded to carry a Church Mouse for a month or two. But the problems have not gone away. If *Veneer* is to emerge from this twilight existence, then it must make the quantum jump into a higher circulation orbit. Few national advertisers show much interest in a publication with a circulation of less than 50,000, and general-consumer advertising (that is, for products unrelated to the magazine's specialty) is unlikely to appear in a publication of under 150,000.

How can this be done?

The simple answer is to imitate Big Store operations and hire a staff capable of exploiting the potential of *Veneer* and acquiring sufficient funds to (1) pay them and (2) finance promotion campaigns for both circulation and advertising. An editor, a circulation director, an ad director, and an art director (doubling as production manager) form a skeleton staff. Let's assume they are dedicated and believe in the future of the magazine; each receives a rock-bottom wage of $30,000 in 1988 dollars. Even then, you have ceased to be a Church Mouse. If, besides being publisher, you are also editor-in-chief then you are likely to need the services of a competent managing editor (another $30,000) and a secretary (part-time at $13,000). The magazine is now in a race for its life. Can you and the new staff drive upward fast enough to outstrip those markedly higher costs, and carry *Veneer* on up to a new plateau of circulation and advertising revenues? The details of such a race are sketched in columns (3) to (6) of the budget table.

Often, however, new magazines cannot stand the pace. Many Church Mice have neither the capital nor the experience for such a breakthrough. So what to do? If, like James Lawrence, you work as a reporter for a local city newspaper you may persuade your colleagues to kick in a couple of good articles for nothing and ask your friends on the business side to help out with advertising and circulation for no more than expenses incurred. Instead of a rented office you may work out of your kitchen or your loft, or persuade someone to let you use that old apartment over the garage. Once again, the appeal of the magazine's editorial concept may be the critical factor in inspiring others to assist you in bringing it to life.

CIRCULATION

If *Veneer* is to stay afloat, it must increase its readership sharply. This is no easy task, since magazines lose between 20 and 50 percent of their old subscribers at the beginning of each new year. To stem this tide and to move forward against it requires a special brand of promotional flair. But *Veneer*'s readers are loyal (70 percent renew), and it is your target to push your circulation to 30,000 by the end of the first year. As an initial move you analyze the demographic differences between the Johnson Tool readers who bought your subscription and those who did not. Are subscribers located in certain geographic districts? Are they city, suburban, or rural dwellers? If you obtain a rough profile of the reader, you can use it to smoke out more readers with the same characteristics.

Perhaps, too, you can tailor your editorial matter to snare a group of peripheral readers. You may discover through the letters column, inquiries, or a small survey that a sizable proportion of those who subscribe are also interested in upholstering furniture. You run some articles on this delicate art, and a profile of a top upholsterer, together with tips of the trade. By expanding your editorial "window" you are pulling in a new group of readers. Another step might be to rent a subscription list of *Upholstery World*, circulation 100,000. But at anything from eight cents to 12 cents a name, this could cost you big bucks. Where can a Church Mouse lay hands on such money? William Blair, the former publisher of *Harper's*, used a neat idea to obtain capital when his *Country Journal* was less than six months old. "Our first issue came out in May 1974 and in October we were in the mails with an advance renewal." About one-quarter of Blair's subscribers sent him money for a second year's subscription when the first year was scarcely half over. When remaining first-year subscriptions came due, readers were encouraged to renew for longer periods, and the up-front money was ploughed back into the operation. In Blair's judgment cash flow — the amount of money moving through the system — is far more important to a new publisher than abstract calculations of profit and loss. "The nub of it," he asserts, "is that you have to have more money coming in than going out."

SPIN-OFFS

The dexterous use of spin-offs is one of the most effective ways for a new publisher to bridge the midstage Chasm. Indeed, it often constitutes the difference between starvation and survival. It depends for its success upon the willing collaboration of the readers. Not long after it began, *Harrowsmith* got into a fierce cash bind. "The printer's bills were going to blow us away," recalls James Lawrence. "Then we had a bright idea. Why not collect the best articles to appear in the magazine and republish them in book form as *The Harrowsmith Reader*? It was the perfect Christmas gift." This one caper brought more than $200,000 into the magazine's coffers. True, a good portion of it went out in expenses, but the boost in cash flow brought it quite a bit closer to the sunlight.

Another gimmick for bridging the gap is to offer specialized books to readers at a slight discount. The magazine then drop-ships the

Table 3
COSTS BY MONTH OF VENEER MAGAZINE

	PILOT ISSUE		END OF YEAR 1		END OF YEAR 2		END OF YEAR 3		END OF YEAR 4		END OF YEAR 5	
	1	2	3	4	5	6	7	8	9	10	11	12
INCOME	DATA	DOLLARS	DATA	DOLLARS	DATA	DOLLARS	DATA	DOLLARS	DATA	DOLLARS	DATA	DOLLARS
Total Printed	19,000		37,000		63,531		108,585		178,794		213,105	
Total Paid Circ.	14,666		29,333		48,699		80,421		127,294		151,605	
Newsstand Price	$3.00/copy		$3.00/copy		$3.00/copy		$3.00/copy		$3.00/copy		$3.00/copy	
Newsstand Sales	1,666	5,000	3,333	10,000	6,666	20,000	13,335	40,005	25,000	75,000	30,000	90,000
Unsold Draw	2,333		6,666		13,334		26,665		50,000		60,000	
Sub Renewals (rate: 70%)	–		9,100		18,200		29,423		46,962		71,605	
Subs from Newstd Conversions at 40%	–		666		1,333		2,666		5,332		10,000	
New Subs, Dir. Mail (% paid up)	13,000		16,234 (11%)		22,500 (9%)		35,000 (7%)		50,000 (5%)		40,000 (4%)	
Total Subscriptions	13,000	32,500	26,000	65,000	42,033	105,083	67,089	167,723	102,294	255,735	121,605	304,012
Subs, Earned Rev per Copy	$2.50		$2.50		$2.50		$2.50		$2.50		$2.50	
Free Promo Copies	1,000		1,000		1,500		1,500		1,500		1,500	
Price, Full-Page Ad	$630		$1,125		$2,025		$3,000		$4,200		$6,000	
Ad Page, less 15% Commission	$535		$956		$1,721		$2,550		$3,570		$5,100	
CPM/Rate Base, 000s	$45/14K		$45/25K		$45/45K		$40/75K		$35/120K		$40/150K	
Ads Sold/Issue	7	3,749	10	9,560	15	25,818	21	53,550	30	107,100	35	178,500
Spin-offs/Book Club/ Loans/Advances	–		74,000	12,333	85,000	14,166	90,000	15,000	96,000	16,000	108,000	18,000
TOTAL INCOME		41,249		96,893		165,067		276,278		453,835		590,512
EXPENSES												
Typeset/Seps/Paper/Printing	80¢/copy	15,200	80¢/copy	29,600	80¢/copy	50,825	80¢/copy	86,868	$1.20/copy	214,553	$1.20/copy	255,726
Commis Newstd Distrib. (50%)	$1.50/copy	2,500	$1.50/copy	5,000	$1.50/copy	10,000	$1.50/copy	20,000	$1.50/copy	37,500	$1.50/copy	45,000
Cost, Subs Fulfil/Mailing	30¢/copy	3,900	30¢/copy	7,800	30¢/copy	12,610	30¢/copy	20,126	30¢/copy	30,688	30¢/copy	36,481

Salaries/Year	$150,000	$25,000	$200,000	33,333	$240,000	40,000	$360,000	60,000	$360,000	60,000	$460,000	76,666
Editorial/Artwork	$36,000	6,000	$42,000	7,000	$54,000	9,000	$72,000	12,000	$96,000	16,000	$120,000	20,000
General Admin/Rent/Phone	$24,000	4,000	$36,000	6,000	$48,000	8,000	$60,000	10,000	$60,000	10,000	$74,000	12,333
Circ. Direct Mail Promo.	$44,274	7,379	$75,000	12,500	$150,000	25,000	$300,000	50,000	$300,000	50,000	$420,000	70,000
%-age Paid Response Applied to Next Year	11%	↑	9%	↑	7%	↑	5%	↑	4%	↑	3%	↑
Ad Sales Promo. Travel/Surveys	6,000	1,000	12,000	2,000	18,000	3,000	30,000	5,000	36,000	6,000	48,000	8,000
Debt Service												
TOTAL EXPENSES		64,979		103,233		158,435		263,994		424,741		524,206
TOTAL ISSUE PROFIT (& LOSS)		[23,730]		[6,339]		6,633		12,284		29,094		66,806
CUMULATIVE PROFIT (& LOSS)		[23,730]		[90,207]		[91,089]		[34,338]		89,796		490,632

EXPLANATORY NOTES, Table 3

1. Unsold draw. Most magazines print more issues than they sell, since the public must see the publication on the newsstands before it can buy. Distribution costs take up 50 percent of newsstand sales.

2. Subscription sales in any year are a total of (a) former subscribers renewing, (b) newsstand readers converting and (c) new readers acquired by direct mail. The subscription price of $15 is prorated over the six issues of the year at $2.50 a copy— designated as "earned revenue per copy."

3. Ad-page price is amount paid by advertiser to ad agency ($630 in Data column, Pilot Issue), which deducts 15% commission before sending remainder to magazine ($535).

4. Mailing and fulfillment amount to 30¢ per copy. Of this, about two-thirds goes to mail, and one-third goes to record keeping and fulfillment of a subscription.

5. Editorial and artwork payments—primarily to free-lancers—increase as quality of product increases. In the same way, production/printing costs increase from 80¢ to $1.20 a copy at end of Year Four as magazine improves paper and print quality.

6. Salaries account more than doubles over four-year period. Some of this is for new help for more complex operation, some is increases for staffers who ate hardtack at the creation. Administration and office costs also increase in like manner.

7. Direct mail solicitations generally cost publisher about $300 per thousand pieces in 1988 dollars. As the lists broaden and become more diffuse, percentages of paying respondents decrease from 11 percent to 9 percent to 7 percent to 5 percent and then 4 percent and 3 percent. These percentages apply to the subscriptions of the following year, hence the arrows.

8. Debt service remains blank because the Church Mouse tends to postpost paying his/her bills 'til the last moment, often waiting for new subscription revenues to pay last year's bills. Here spin-offs, strong cash flow, and the allure of the publisher's concept, are of critical importance in bridging this financial chasm.

9. Cumulative totals in Profit (Loss) carried from year to year are computed on the basis of the average profit/loss between one year and the next.

requests to the book publishers, skimming 30 to 45 percent off the top in the process.

With this in mind you decide to publish the *Best of Veneer* (price $18) and the *Veneer Handbook of Furniture Restoration* (price $25). By the end of the first year they bring you $150,000 half of which goes to production and sales expenses for the books and the other half of which you use to defray operating costs (see table 3, "Spin-offs," columns 3 and 4) and to help boost circulation into the higher orbit for the succeeding year (see columns 5 and 6). You purchase the readership lists of *Uphol-stery World* and *Masterpiece* for a major direct mail appeal. You also place ads for *Veneer* subscribers in a number of other publications with possible crossover appeal. As you move through the second year your circulation rises to some 49,000 but as the lists broaden, they become more diffuse, and the proportion of paid-up responses falls year by year from 9 percent to 7 percent and then to 5 percent. Newsstand sales, however, steadily increase from 3,300 to 6,600 to 13,300 (see columns 3, 5, and 7), and 40 percent of these use their insert cards to become full-time subscribers. In the same fashion, each year 70 percent of the previous year's readers renew their subscriptions, to give *Veneer* a total paid circulation of 80,000 by the end of the magazine's third year.

As *Veneer*'s circulation increases, its readership becomes of growing interest to advertisers. For the pilot issue the ad director sold the equivalent of seven full-page ads. By the end of the first year he has increased this to ten pages. But a glance at the foot of column 2 shows clearly that this is not enough to cover expenses. So much so that by the end of the first year (see the foot of column 4) *Veneer* has accumulated, on paper at least, obligations of some $90,000. By the end of the second year (see foot of column 6) this deficit has swollen to $91,000.

SQUEAKING THROUGH

How, the aspiring publisher may wonder, can a new and untried organization shoulder such a burden of debt and survive? Good question. Many do not. These early days provide the ultimate test of the Church Mouse's ability to "squeak" through. First, the publisher of *Veneer* had the foresight to reduce the number of issues per year from twelve to six, or "6X" as they say in the trade. If he or she had not, the debt would have piled up at twice the speed. The Church Mouse's second great survival skill is the ability to create credit by *prevarication*. Not all bills have to be paid on time. Some can be paid one, two, or even three months late. Generally, creditors find such burdens easier to bear if the Church Mouse levels with them and explains what is happening and how much brighter are the prospects ahead.

Of course, the "don't-pay-til-the-invoices-turn-pink" strategy is a double-edged sword. *Veneer*'s own creditors may play the same game. Payments for newsstand sales and from advertisers may take six months, or even a year, to come in. Many magazines estimate that up to 10 percent of their advertisers' bills will prove uncollectible.

Despite such hazards, however, the situation for *Veneer*, as displayed in the table, may not be as critical as it seems. During the first year the accumulation of $90,000 in debt is cushioned by two factors. The $195,000 in upfront subscription revenues (not fully shown in column 2) is likely to shield *Veneer* from its obligations until issue no. 4 is in production. By then revenue from the book club and the new subscriptions from direct mail solicitations will be flowing into the system. Similarly, as the new debts are carried into the second year, they will be covered, after some delay, by a new wave of subscription renewals, and more advertising on a broadened rate base. As Bill Blair points out, the key to the Church Mouse's continued survival is cash flow.

ADVERTISING SALES

How does the ad director determine the price of a page of advertising? Obviously, it must be a function of paid circulation. A publication with a large circulation must be able to charge more than one with a small circulation. But it is also a function of reader "quality," his or her ability to spend a lot or a little on the products advertised. It is for this reason that the manufacturer of a Mercedes car is prepared to pay more to reach 1,000 of his potential customers than the brewer of Treadmill beer is prepared to pay to reach 1,000 of his potential customers. When your ad director is attempting to figure how much she should charge advertisers per page, she will glance at the prices being charged by competitors like *Upholstery World*. This publication, she learns from *Standard Rates and Data* (5201 Old Orchard Rd., Skokie, Ill. 60077), charges its advertisers $4,500 for a full-page ad. But its circulation is 100,000 and *Veneer*'s is only 25,000. What must *Veneer* charge for an ad to be competitive? If it costs $4,500 to reach 100,000 readers, then it costs $45 to reach 1,000 readers. The competitive price for a magazine with a circulation of 25,000 then becomes

25 times $45, or $1,125 (see column 3). This rate, or cost per thousand readers, is referred to in the trade as the CPM.

An advertiser can learn a great deal about a magazine by checking its CPM. Most mass-circulation magazines have relatively low CPMs. In 1987 *TV Guide* (circulation 17 million) had a CPM of $5.30 and *National Geographic* (10 million) had a CPM of $9.30. In contrast, *Business Week* had a CPM of $60.80 and *Ms.* had a CPM of $25.90. The consumer books would like to charge more per thousand readers, but they cannot since their readership is so huge and so diverse that much of the ad's impact is scattered shotgun fashion among the readers who never buy auto batteries or never smoke cigarettes. In contrast, the smaller magazines with their riflelike approach to their highly specialized readerships can offer much more fertile ground for the advertiser, and therefore charge quite a bit more per thousand readers.

Veneer is clearly a specialized publication. At $45 its CPM is competitive, but the ad director would like to steal a march on *Upholstery World* by reducing it first to $40 and then to $35. She knows, however, that while this might give *Veneer* an apparent edge, its low circulation base would probably prove unattractive to the bigger advertisers. *Veneer's* ad director will then probably find herself riding the circulation director hard to expand readership to 100,000 and beyond during the next year. The circulation director agrees that this is a fine and noble place to be, but warns that it is going to cost another $150,000 in promotion to get there.

Some publishers have been known to remortgage their homes or farms to raise the money. But perhaps there are some intermediate measures you can try before taking this ultimate step. Maybe you can talk to your old friends down at Johnson Tool Co. and get them to put together *Veneer's Complete Furniture Finishing Kit* and promote it through the magazine. The price, with sanders and lacquers, will be $125, giving you a profit of $40 for every item sold. Or perhaps you can strengthen your magazine's finances (and credibility) by establishing an awards contest for the best restored furniture of the year in five categories. Top contenders are winnowed out by four authorities in the field, and prizes of $1,000 cash are presented by a major paint company, together with a replica of a miniature Chippendale chair fashioned in pewter. The honors are conferred at the Veneer Restoration Awards Banquet ($50 per couple for Chicken à la King and a glass of cheap plonk; the magazine takes back the difference). Yes, you are deep in huckster country now, but you know it is all for a good cause.

If the finances for your new circulation drive are still unavailable, you might work out a deal with your printer. Right now he has a monthly printing bill of about $87,000. If you can push your circulation to 120,000, and improve quality, this would more than double (see columns 8 and 10). If the printer will not underwrite your bank loan, then perhaps you can use a neat gambit employed by Bernard Goldhirsh when he was navigating *Sail* across the Chasm. Goldhirsh first persuaded his printer to send him a letter demanding assurance of payment, and then took this to his bank and asked them, on the strength of his predictable advertising and subscription receipts, to guarantee the payment of his printing bills should he default. The bank granted it. With this guarantee in place, the printers were confident enough to let *Sail's* bills go unpaid for six months while Goldhirsh had $500,000 in freed funds to play into his new drive for readers and advertising.

You increase your direct mail expenditures from $150,000 to $300,000 during the third and fourth years (see columns 7 and 9), and *Veneer's* paid circulation climbs from 80,000 to 127,000 and then to 151,000. But you are not out of shoal water yet. Even though you have reduced your CPM to $40 and then to $35 in order to look competitive to the big advertisers who normally work with *Upholstery World* and *Masterpiece*, there is still an element of loss. True, you increase the number of ad pages per issue from twenty-one to thirty, but the smaller advertisers who helped you squeak through the early days can no longer afford page rates of $3,000 and $4,000. Some cut back to half a page, and others melt away, feeling that you have suddenly become too rich for their blood. This leaves a nasty taste in your mouth so you summon your ad director. How can we keep our old friends on board? Why not, he suggests, take care of the needs of the smaller advertisers by instituting a regional advertising insert; this will give them reasonable rates and tight targeting for their products.

By the end of the fourth year *Veneer* has paid off its accumulated debt, and each issue is generating net revenues of $29,000. Twelve months later this figure has risen to nearly $67,000 an issue. You are not rich yet. But you are the publisher of a magazine with a proven record and everything seems possible! Perhaps you will use the additional cash flow to take *Veneer* 12X; or — and this is generally a sounder policy for a Church Mouse — you might generate a concept for a second magazine and use the combined resources of the Veneer Publishing Co. to produce issues of each on alternate months.

As a Church Mouse you have depended for your success on the drawing power of your idea, the goodwill of your friends, and the generosity and good faith of your printer and your banker. Most important of all, however, your success depended upon your ability to attract the interest of your readers and then enlist them as active partners in the struggle to bring the new magazine across the financial Chasm. Each reader may have only a few dollars to spend, but collectively an ardent readership presents a source of overwhelming financial strength.

"*Harrowsmith* created much of its special relationship with readers by telling them of our behind-the-scenes problems," says James Lawrence. "We printed some highly critical letters, particularly on the subject of our attitude to advertising. Our friends said this was a suicidal policy but, in retrospect, it really made readers feel that they had a say in how we evolved."

Every new magazine is different. But clearly, if the readership lacks this fealty of shared endeavor, no publication can succeed. With it, most aspiring publishers will find it hard to fail.

13

BUILDING A CAREER
How to Be Lucky

WHEN THE NAME OF AN OFFICER was recommended to Napoleon to lead a new military campaign, the great commander did not ask if that officer knew about cavalry tactics or the role of artillery. Bonaparte's first query was *"Est-ce qu'il est heureux?"* Is he lucky? The answer to the question was, for him, by far the best indicator of how that campaign might fare.

Why do some people get ahead and build immensely satisfying and lucrative careers and others of comparable talent stay pretty much in place? Is it luck? Did the others just get a raw deal? Or is there something in the outlook or attitude of the winners that distinguishes them from the losers? Clearly, Bonaparte thought there was. "Is he lucky?" is not an inquiry about the laws of chance but about the nature of a person's character.

Present-day studies have confirmed this Napoleonic insight. Even before experience has reinforced the traits, people who deem themselves to be "lucky" or "unlucky" have distinctly different psychological profiles. This is undoubtedly true in the world of communications and, I suspect, in most other professional disciplines. Max Gunther, in his book *The Luck Factor*, cites a survey of the Princeton class of 1949 made a quarter-century after graduation. Mental attitude and not intrinsic ability was the key factor that distinguished the top two-fifths of the class from the bottom fifth.

Napoleon's concept of luck, while useful, has obvious limitations in that it is hitched to the idea of victorious campaigns for the French army. The purpose of this chapter is to help readers to be lucky in a broader sense. Call it the Princeton definition of luck if you like. Will you

167

be able to look back twenty-five years from now and say "I was lucky"? Each individual builds a career and ascends a ladder of development that is unique to him or her alone. There are always adverse twists, a firing or two, but if on the whole what you achieve pleases you, then you have succeeded. If, on the other hand, you find yourself saying, along with the bottom fifth of Princeton's class of 1949, "If only I could do it over again," or "My one chance and I blew it," then you have all the ingredients of a major personal tragedy.

Each year the seventy-five graduates (B.A. and M.A.) of the Magazine sequence at Syracuse University get jobs in the field of journalism. We are proud of our record of full employment. But we don't have any special clout with managing editors. Nor do we attempt to blackmail our middle-aged grads, by now in positions of responsibility, into hiring this year's crop. We do seek, however, to give each student a "lucky" approach to the job market. The first step in this is to have each of them ask two important questions:

1. What kind of job do I want to be doing ten or fifteen years from now? Managing editor of *San Franciso*? Fashion editor of *McCall's*? Associate editor at *Sports Illustrated*? Or what?

2. What is the gateway for that position? Where do I start?

It is axiomatic that you must have a plan if you are to act in an intelligent fashion. Yet surprisingly few people have a plan, or have taken the trouble to sit down, put their heads in their hands, and really *think* about what they'd like to be doing with their lives. I stress the importance of ambition. Students, perhaps because of all the red ink they get on their assignment papers, tend to underestimate their abilities. Yet, if you don't have dreams — and state them clearly to yourself — those dreams can never come true.

To illustrate this process, let's see how a young graduate — perhaps you — might build a satisfying and lucrative career in the world of magazines. Your name, for the purposes of the exercise, will be John M. Dokes. You are in your early twenties. One day close to graduation, you sit down in front of a cup of strong coffee, put your head in your hands, and really *think* about what you'd like to be doing in fifteen years' time.

After much consideration, you decide you want to be the managing editor of *Savant* magazine. It has a circulation of 3 million, it comes out monthly, and it is editorially a cross between *Playboy* and *Harper's*, with a fair number of future-oriented articles in the style of *Omni*. The next step, for many first-time job aspirants, seems obvious. You type up a résumé (more about this in a moment) and mail it in to the editor of *Savant* with a request for a job. It is unlikely the editor will write back,

but in a few days you may get a note from the magazine's personnel director inviting you in for an interview. Your spirits soar, but you quickly
discover that the only positions available for someone with your slender
experience are minor administrative jobs with almost no real editorial responsibilities. Many novices are hooked into such positions on the assurance that they will one day "work their way up to associate editor." All
too often, however, when the full-time editorial slot opens up (two or three
years from now) it is likely to be filled by someone from outside the magazine. Why? For the last two years you have not been honing your editorial
skills; you have channeled your energies into administrative duties. You
have, in short, just learned the hard way that a direct lunge at a responsible editorial position is a bit like a direct lunge at happiness: chances
are your bucket will come up empty.

A FOOT IN THE DOOR

A more careful analysis shows that the entry gateway for the managing
editorship of *Savant* lies elsewhere. Your research shows you that some
of that magazine's writers and editors come from *Newsweek* and *Discover*,
but you find that most came up through such general-interest magazines
as *Fantastic* and *Terrific*, both with circulations between half a million and
a million. These, in turn, seem to hire most of their staffers from small
specialized magazines and medium-sized newspapers, who hire from small
dailies and weeklies. Your gateway problem, then, has become one of getting hired by such a newspaper. Sometimes getting hired on a small-town
newspaper is a breeze. But more often, particularly if you are a newcomer
to journalism, you may have to use your utmost powers of persuasion.
And, if these fail, you may have to employ the subtle reportorial device
of jamming your foot in the door.

  Best prospects for this kind of operation are in your hometown
since there is sometimes a slight editorial resistance to carpetbaggers. You
live in Gleanville, so you write to Mrs. Georgia Bloggs, the editor of the
Gleanville Monitor (daily circulation 18,000) and enclose a résumé. This
is a Worst-Case Scenario, so you get no immediate reply, and you call her.

   "Mrs. Bloggs?"
   "Yup."
   "Did you get my letter and résumé?"
   "Who are you?"

"Dokes, ma'am, John Dokes."

"Look, John, I'm on a deadline." Click.

Moral: Find out from Mrs. Bloggs's secretary when the deadlines are and work around them. If she doesn't have a secretary, ask her right off if she's on a deadline, and if so when you should call back. Let's try again.

"Mrs. Bloggs?"

"Yup."

"Are you on a deadline?"

"Nope."

"I'm John Dokes. Did you get my letter . . ."

"Yup. But we don't have any openings. Sorry."

"But could I come by to say Howdy, so you'll know me when something comes up?"

"Sure. Three o'clock tomorrow." Click.

When you see Mrs. Bloggs you can ask her what she looks for when she hires a new reporter. She'll tell you, maybe describing a new gateway in the process.

"We generally require a couple of years on a weekly somewhere before we hire. Gotta have clippings." You show her your scant assemblage and she leafs through them without much interest. You try again.

"Do you take any free-lance stuff?"

"Nope." (Remember, this is the Worst-Case Scenario. But now it's time to jam your foot in the door.)

"But you are interested in story ideas, events, and things going on around Gleanville?"

"What editor wouldn't be?"

"Can I bounce some off you now?"

"Sure. But we don't pay much."

"Here are three ideas. A man in East Gleanville just opened a blacksmith shop. He does everything from shoeing horses to fixing wrought-iron gates, and now he's making chandeliers from his own designs . . . Great picture possibilities. . . ."

"Maybe . . . what else you got?"

After a couple of months' free-lancing for Mrs. Bloggs you'll have a nice clippings file, and maybe a few bylines. You'll be working full-time stacking pallets down at the warehouse, or stacking books in the library, but nobody said breaking in was a breeze. The first big break comes when Mrs. Bloggs hires you as her new reporter, and your energies can now be concentrated on the job in hand. Soon you write a series or two. They are picked up by the wire services. You win a press-club award and an interview with the managing editor of the *Zenith Bulletin* (circulation 200,000 daily). You are on your way.

A year or two on a daily newspaper is not just good preparation for future managing editors of *Savant*. It forms an excellent gateway for just about every known job in the world of magazines. I have gone into some detail on your dealings with Mrs. Bloggs because of all the quantum jumps you are likely to negotiate in your career, this is undoubtedly the most spectacular. Before, you were an odd-job person. After, you are a professional, with a trade and an earned stool at the press club bar.

In that first year you learn to get your typewriter (or VDT) around a simple declarative sentence, and then hitch it together with other similar sentences. You learn to live with deadlines, and take them in stride. You also learn to get along with a Hogarthian panorama of social types. Mike Kranish, a former student of mine, went to work for a small newspaper in Florida after graduation. One day he was trading wisecracks with a couple of jailed bookies down at the courthouse, and the next he found himself in a one-on-one interview with the man who was shortly to become president of the United States. At first such contrasts leave you dazed and dazzled. Then you get into the swing of things. Deadline panic broils out of your system like fat out of a steak. A plane crashes at the airport, and it's 10 minutes to deadline. Five minutes on the phone, checking the facts. Three minutes for writing, one for checking your copy, and one for leaning back, feet on desk, to light your stogie.

RÉSUMÉ

A newspaper job forms an elegant springboard for vaulting onto the staff of medium-sized magazines. Do you want to work for *Ski* or *Psychology Today*? Perhaps there is a top skier in your region who'd made a good profile. Or perhaps a psychologist at a nearby university has come up with a new study on high school sex mores. You sell the story, then a few more like it and — next time that magazine has an opening, it'll want to see your résumé.

The first thing to remember about going for any job is to ask yourself what you can do for the editor, and only secondarily what he or she can do for you. It is surprising how many potential hires switch off their would-be employer by getting the order reversed. The second thing to remember about going for a job is that it is not the purpose of the résumé to get you hired; its purpose, plain and simple, is to convince some editor that you are worth hauling in for an interview (at company expense). It is in the interview that you display your sunny disposition and your clips — these are what get you the job. If you accept this stripped-down version of the résumé, then a lot of things fall into place. Here are some pointers (and see figure 29) that you will find helpful in preparing a résumé appropriate for most jobs in journalism:

1. The résumé should be neatly typed and duplicated. Most universities have access to laser printing services. Elaborate printing jobs smack of PR, which makes some editors uneasy.

2. It should be short, and kept to a single page. Editors are busy people and want to get to the point.

3. Make it easy to read. Break it into three major sections: *Personal, Education* and *Professional Experience,* followed by a small section on hobbies. Lead each section with the best, and work back. Dates go at the end of the line (see figure 29).

4. Strip out all achievements unrelated to the job. Nobody cares if you chaired the college dance marathon, unless you are applying for a job at *Dance* magazine.

5. Aim it at giving the reader a sense of momentum, so that the next logical step becomes your employment. If necessary, rewrite each résumé to precisely target the kind of job you seek.

6. Good journalists tend to have interesting hobbies; they often form the sources of many good story ideas. Remember, editors are not just hiring a technician; they are hiring a human being — one who, they hope, will be a congenial person to work with. If you don't have any outside interests at all, then perhaps you are in the wrong business altogether.

INTERVIEW

The résumé goes in to *Fantastic* magazine, and a couple of weeks later you are invited in for a interview. Unless the circumstances are weird, the publication should pay the freight. First impressions are important. Arrive with time to spare, but don't present yourself to the secretary more than 5 minutes ahead of time. Make sure you have read back issues of *Fantastic* for the last year. If a story is mentioned in discussion, you can *subtly* show you've done your homework. "I loved that thing on the Buddhist truck driver — how did you get him to sit still for that?" This isn't apple polishing; you are simply showing your familiarity with the product and its style of doing business.

Whole books have been written about effective job interviewing

RÉSUMÉ
of
John M. Dokes

Address:
17 North Lane
Gleanville, Ames 40729

Phone: (349) 555-4567

PERSONAL

Age: 24

Health: excellent

Photo attached

(Marital status: single)

EDUCATION

B.A. History & Political Science, Waindell College, 1986
Grade point 3.4 out of 4
Three years Dean's list
Rotary Scholarship $600

Gleanville High School, 19th in class of 320, graduated 1982
Member Photo Club, Debate Club
Spent summer 1975 Grenoble, France

Speak fair French

PROFESSIONAL EXPERIENCE

Reporter, *Zenith Bulletin* (circulation 200,000 daily) 1987–present

Reporter, copy editor, *Gleanville Monitor* (circ. 18,000) 1986–87

Reporter, features editor, *Waindell Dude* (circ. 4,000) 1983–86

Assistant editor, *Gleanville Gleaner* (circ. 400) 1981–82

Published articles: "Self before Sex," *Psychology Today,* 1987
"Uphill Champ," *Ski* magazine, 1986

Series entitled "City Government: A Necessary Evil" in seven parts for *Monitor,*
won Merks Award and prize $100

SPECIAL INTERESTS include:

Cross-country skiing, photography, hot-air ballooning, French cooking, the blues of Blind Lemon Jefferson

Fig. 29. Sample résumé.

and I am not going to traverse the ground again. Interviews for jobs in journalism tend to be refreshingly free of conmanship; probably more than in any other profession, editors are interested in on-the-job performance, not social pirouettes. If they ask you to take a writing test, jump at it. If they ask you to take a typing test think twice; you may be lurching over into the wrong track. If they ask you to take a psychological profile, go along with it if you want the job badly enough. But you're getting a clear signal; this organization is under the command not of editors but of manic personnel persons. For all its tidy management, the publication is probably a lackluster editorial product. Reason? Good writers produce spacy Rorschachs.

Robert Townsend, in his delightful book *Up the Organization*, has identified two primary forms, or ways, in which human beings can operate as a group. What he calls the Theory-Y organization is set up for individuals who are not status-oriented but intent upon achieving some goal beyond the continued existence of the group. The tone is informal and people-oriented. In contrast, the Theory-X organization (Townsend includes the Catholic Church and the Roman Army as examples of this type) exists to perpetuate the status and power of the leaders at the expense of the followers. Wherever you work, your publication will form an organization and perhaps be part of a yet bigger organization. Even in a short visit you can get some good hints about whether you are into a dead Theory-X or a lively Theory-Y setup.

Here are four pointers for detecting Theory-X organizations:

1. When you call your intended boss on the phone and that individual is never at his or her desk but "in conference." Why is so much time spent in conference? Simple. Such individuals are not empowered to make decisions about anything; all decisions are nice, safe, group decisions, made in conference.

2. If you have to interview more than one (at the outside two) individuals, you are deep into X-country. No single person has the authority to make a decision about you. It is likely a communal operation with an ill-defined sense of what is good work and what is not. Sometimes this is fine, but sometimes it is deadly.

3. Do a horseback check of relations between the upper and lower levels of the staff. Do the peons seem cheerful in their work? Do bosses, after an amiable argument — say, over an art layout — change their minds? Keep in mind that even when secretaries — male or female — first-name bosses, this is not always a sign of high morale.

4. If the head honcho has a whole phalanx of secretaries outside the door, beware. They are being used for status; an efficient boss would have delegated all that labor away to other departments.

As an editor of *Business Week* it was my lot to interview many of the nation's top businesspeople. The efficient, productive ones never had more than one secretary. And dear old Bob Townsend, when he was chairman of Avis Rent-a-Car, made a point of having no secretary at all. This, I suspect, was a triumph of theory over practicality; I had it on the sly from his colleagues that he used *their* secretaries quite a bit.

Let us continue to follow the rise of you (alias John Dokes) through the infrastructure of journalism. Dick Lobe, the managing editor of *Fantastic* (circulation 600,000, editorial general interest aimed at active younger set) is interested in hiring you. But he is cagey about paying you more than he needs to. The dialogue goes like this:

"How much do you want?"

"In salary?"

"Yes."

"Well . . ."

If you say $26,000 and you later find out you could have gotten $28,000, you'll feel a mug. But if you ask for $28,000, the managing editor may only have $24,000 and you'll have priced yourself out of the market. To reply, "Oh, you decide what's fair" is disturbingly passive. "I'll take anything I can get" sounds a little too hungry. Perhaps the best response is another question.

"How much do you want?" asks Lobe.

"Salary? What's the bracket you have on that position?"

"Between $24,000 and $29,000."

"Well, I've got quite a bit of experience, and I'm not up on your local cost of living. It must be quite a bit higher than Zenith's."

"How about $26,000?"

"As I said, there are so many imponderables. Frankly, I think $27,000 would be nearer the mark."

"Geez. Okay, but I'll have to confirm with the publisher."

You were shrewd not to push your future managing editor to the limit of $29,000. You might have gotten it, or gotten closer to it, but it would substantially increase the pressure on you, the new kid, to perform as a wunderkind. This way you can make a couple of bloops and still bounce back.

For the next eighteen months you work hard and effectively. You come up with some great story ideas, and find bright people to write them. You show that you can edit personality profiles and trends alike under pressure of a tight deadline. In short, everything is clicking along nicely except that your salary doesn't seem to be coming up very fast. Despite assurances that things will improve, they do not. Finally, you corner Dick Lobe in his office.

"How much do you want?"

"I was thinking $30,000."

"No way."

"I got the Maggie Chisholm column, and we nailed the Wicker Award for the South Africa piece . . ."

"Forget it, John. You've done good work, sure, but everybody does good work. They wouldn't be at *Fantastic* magazine if they didn't . . . and you've presided over your share of screw-ups."

"Yeah, the November issue."

"And there was the chimneysweep profile . . . you know, John, I've been meaning to talk to you about how things are going for you here at *Fantastic* and whether you're really happy here."

"You want to unload me?"

"No, Johnny, but at $30,000 you're too rich for our blood."

It is hard to believe but this dialogue, or one very much like it, takes place several times a year at just about every magazine in the country. If you are not ambitious it may not happen to you. But if you are, it assuredly will, sooner rather than later. If you understand the underlying dynamics of the putdown or Deflator that the editor just administered to his employee, then you will be in a far better position to combat this kind of thing when you ask your own boss for a raise, and make any of the other shrewd moves necessary to maximize your potential and build the kind of "lucky" career you want for yourself. Crazy though this dialogue may seem, it has a sequel that is crazier still. It is set in the same office, one month later.

"Come in, John. What's on your mind?"

"It's about our talk last month, Dick."

"Yeah?"

"It seems you're not too wild about my work at *Fantastic* . . ."

"For an assistant editor you're good, John, but not great."

"Anyway, after our talk I went over to see Susan Warchek at *Terrific* and she's offered me an associate editorship, and I'm here now to give you notice."

"*Terrific*, eh?" Lobe seems unfazed. "How much are they offering, Jacko?"

"$34,000."

"Big bucks. But no sweat, we can easily match that."

"Match it?" You are nonplussed. "A month ago you wouldn't spring for $30,000."

"We really appreciate your talent around here, Johnny. Maybe I overdid it. Just the other day I told Charlie, 'That John's a real comer.'

Stick around, my friend. Who knows, one day you may be sitting behind this desk . . ."

You are perplexed. On the face of it the dialogue is not just crazy, it's plain dumb. Why does Dick Lobe pay a good person less than he's worth, drive him onto the open market, then try to retain him at a substantially higher salary than originally requested?

It is hard to make any sense of the above scenario until you realize that Dick Lobe — despite his $90,000-a-year salary — is not sitting on Mount Olympus. He is, in fact, also a lowly hireling with a seat quite a bit hotter than your own. The publisher of *Fantastic* has determined that Lobe shall have only so many assistant editor positions with a salary bracket of $24,000 to $29,000. You are making $28,500 now and want $30,000. Lobe may agree with you that you are worth $30,000, but if he pays it he will get hell from the publisher, who now has to sell more ads to cover it and — in a little while — similar raises for the other deserving assistant editors. The publisher values Lobe for his ability to hire the necessary talent for the lowest reasonable cost. If the price of staying within the salary brackets is keeping his editors a little off-balance with a Deflator talk or two, then Lobe will probably pay it, offensive though the task may be to his post-Nixonian soul.

The "don't-get-too-big-for-your-breeches" talks can have one of two effects. They either leave you subdued and happy to have any kind of job at all at *Fantastic.* Or they nettle your pride, as happened with you in the role of John Dokes, and make you hustle out in search of something better. If you are good enough, then you will probably get a nice offer. How then can Lobe the Tightfisted turn into Lobe the Profligate without irking the publisher? The answer is clear. You have surprised Dick by proving your talents are apparently worth $34,000 to a competing publication. If the publisher is to retain your services and perhaps put them to work in a more responsible position, then Lobe must be able to get out and pay the going rate. That, as they say, is the price of doing business.

In truth, Lobe made a couple of miscalculations about John. But they were both minor. He did not believe John could get a better job at *Terrific.* And he thought he could keep him in place with a matching counteroffer. But John's departure may also be the price of doing business; though he didn't buy the managing editor's Deflator, other editors probably did, and Dick Lobe was able to retain their services at existing rates.

A final comment. No doubt some genuine criticism will be coming your way sooner or later. You should take great care to distinguish it from the Deflator talk. If the managing editor is a plausible soul — and most are — it may be almost impossible to do so. Either way, do *not* call him or her on it. Just go out and get another offer. If you can't, then his or her criticisms might be amply justified. As a general operating procedure, however, it makes sense to save your pitch for a raise for a moment when the editor is complimenting you on some recent effort.

You will recall that it was your original goal (as John Dokes) to become managing editor of *Savant* magazine. Dick Lobe has hinted that you might succeed him in his position, which would surely be a fine springboard for the position at *Savant*. Should you accept *Fantastic*'s counteroffer and work up within the organization? Or will you find greater happiness as an associate editor over at *Terrific*? Answer: Take the new job. It will take several months of hard work to really get in gear at *Terrific* (and you may get fired if things don't work out!) but you will be acquiring valuable new experience. Dick Lobe sounded enthusiastic about keeping you at *Fantastic*, but if you had stuck around as a $34,000 associate editor you might come to sense a little frost in the air. (This guy's good, but is he worth all *that*?)

After three or four years at *Terrific* you may be ready to make your pitch to *Savant*. It's smart to let them know ahead of time that you are interested, so if something opens up you have a chance to make a pitch. Most good jobs at this level don't just appear in your gunsights; you generally have to stalk them with charm and patience. Remember the old maxim — it is worthy of Bonaparte himself: Risk equals danger multiplied by time. Turning this around, we get: good jobs equal meritorious availability multiplied by time. As every house-hunter knows, the longer you stay with it, the greater the chance of finding that perfect place.

Perhaps you will accomplish your dream and become the managing editor and even the editor-in-chief of *Savant*. If you do, then Osborn Elliott, who occupied similar positions at *Newsweek* through the turbulent 1960s and 1970s, has some useful advice on being boss in his autobiography *The World of Oz*:

> Even though I was only in my mid-thirties when I became editor of *Newsweek*, I had already spent a number of years working for a lot of bosses. What had I learned? What I *hope* I learned was: the importance of kindness. The idiocy of arrogance. The virtues of boldness. The pettiness of cruelty. The need for self-assurance. And, above all, the uses of humor.

Nice though that position at *Savant* seems, something else may happen to you (and John Dokes) on your way up the slippery pole. Susan Warchek, the editor-in-chief of *Terrific*, may be so impressed with your work that she makes you chief travel editor, a job that suits you perfectly. When you glance again at *Savant* it does not seem quite so rosy. Another look and you realize that you have the ultimate job right where you are. Your objectives and values may have changed since you first sat down with your head in your hands on graduation day and wondered what you wanted to be doing in fifteen years. It was important that you stated some goal — almost any goal — at that time. Without it, your movement would have remained haphazard and directionless. But now you've worked hard at your career. You have a proven record that you can parlay into some new line of endeavor if you choose. So, if your interests have changed, don't fight it. Go with the flow. Such evolutions are part of living the "lucky" life.

The survey of the Princeton class of 1949 cited by Max Gunther shows that the fifth of the class who felt most disappointed in their expectations shared one central characteristic. They were unwilling to take chances. Many had only worked for one company, or started one venture, in their lives. "The unlucky fifth," declares Gunther, "lacked boldness."

In contrast, all the individuals who had moved boldly in their lives (had held six or more jobs since graduation) felt that they had been lucky. They had not let themselves be smothered in a corner. When they felt boxed in — as John Dokes felt after his Deflator talk — they did not hunker down and hope for the best. They hustled out and found something better. Boldness, of course, has its risks. Sometimes the brave win the fair. But sometimes they just get a bullet in the head. When all the speculation is over, however, each of us still owes God a death. Shall we go as mice? Or shall we buckle up and ride through the Highland glens at the side of the Marquis of Montrose (1612–1650)?

> He either fears his fate too much
> Or his deserts are small
> Who dares not put it to the touch
> To gain or lose it all.

If John Dokes' move to *Terrific* had not worked out, he would have been fired. In a sense, getting fired is the end of the world. But it happens a lot. Even Oz Elliott, the great editor of *Newsweek*, was eventually fired by Katherine Graham. One business magazine's survey of top executives (salaries of $250,000 and up) showed that each, on average, had been fired at least twice. Many firings occur for incompetence. (Is the company doing more for the employee than the employee is doing for the company?) But perhaps an even larger number occur because of a clash of personality or the feeling of new managers — who sometimes have not even met the victim — that they want to staff the operation with "their own people."

Often a firing can be a blessing in disguise. If one is fired for personal style or incompetence, clearly something was wrong. Sometimes you get a better position in the same field. But sometimes it enables you to discover talents you did not know you had. The engineer becomes a magazine editor. The magazine editor starts her own newsletter, which blossoms into a glossy publication. But a firing also develops self-confidence. If you acquire a boss who's a stinker, the knowledge that you can get another job will stiffen your backbone. Oz Elliott describes such an incident in *The World of Oz* when he was a junior writer at *Time*. A senior editor named Joe Purtell (a pure-bred Gargoyle; see chapter 4) made Elliott rewrite a cover story on an auto company four times and still found it unsatisfactory.

> That did it. I marched into Purtell's office, told him I'd been around long enough not to have to take that kind of crap from him. And from then on working relations improved.

If such a showdown does not cause things to improve, you know you can get something more congenial elsewhere. Make a point, however, of getting the new job lined up before telling your old boss to take a walk.

Having the confidence, and the professional skill, to tell any boss to get lost and still come out ahead may be a pretty good definition of what it is to be a "lucky" man or woman. You are master or mistress of your fate and captain of your soul. Perhaps there is great wisdom in the ambiguity of the French word *heureux*.

Good luck. And, as they said back in the bad old Thirties, write when you get work.

INDEX

181

MAGAZINE EDITING FOR PROFESSIONALS

was composed in 10 on 12 Palatino on Digital Compugraphic equipment
by Metricomp;
printed by sheet-fed offset on 55-pound, acid-free, Glatfelter B-16,
and notch bound with paper covers
by Edwards Brothers Incorporated;
with paper covers printed in 2 colors
by Edwards Brothers Incorporated;
designed by Sara L. Eddy;
and published by

SYRACUSE UNIVERSITY PRESS
SYRACUSE, NEW YORK 13244-5160